Stephen Spender

Twayne's English Authors Series

Kinley E. Roby, Editor

Northeastern University

TEAS 491

Stephen Spender

Sanford Sternlicht

Syracuse University

Twayne Publishers • New York
Maxwell Macmillan Canada • Toronto
Maxwell Maxmillan International • New York Oxford Singapore Sydney

Stephen Spender
Sanford Sternlicht

Twayne Publishers   Maxwell Macmillan Canada, Inc.
Macmillan Publishing Company   1200 Eglinton Avenue East
866 Third Avenue   Suite 200
New York, New York 10022   Don Mills, Ontario M3C 3N1

Macmillan Publishing Company is part of the Maxwell Communication Group of
Companies.

Library of Congress Cataloging-in-Publication Data
Sternlicht, Sanford V.
    Stephen Spender / Sanford Sternlicht.
        p.   cm. — (Twayne's English authors series ; TEAS 491)
    Includes bibliographical references (p.   ) and index.
    ISBN 0-8057-7009-7
    1. Spender, Stephen, 1909–   —Criticism and interpretation.
I. Title. II. Series.
PR6037.P47Z86   1992   91-33733
                                                                          CIP

The paper used in this publication meets the minimum
requirements of American National Standard for Information Sciences—Permanence
of Paper for Printed Library Materials. ANSI Z3948-1984. ∞™

10 9 8 7 6 5 4 3 2 1

Printed in the United States of America

Contents

Preface

Elton E. Smith has called them, by way of book title, *The Angry Young Men of the Thirties*: W. H. Auden, Louis MacNeice, C. Day Lewis, and Stephen Spender. These writers of the Proletarian Decade may be the last British poets to have used their art as an expression of political sympathy and solidarity with the oppressed and the impoverished. Sir Stephen Spender still does. It may also be that they were the last generation of British poets who when young made news and whose poetry was widely read. Old sailors who manned square-riggers had a saying for going aloft in stormy weather: "One hand for the ship and one for myself." The thirties poets maintained such a dual commitment to art and to personal life throughout the demoniac decade and then shifted for themselves. Except for Spender, who did not forget.

Spender is a protean writer in quiet control, existentially stoic, first conjecturing and then denying the possibility of a charitable future. He has made a career of confession. Indeed, he may be the most candid of all English writers. Because he has always "tried to do the right thing," one cannot help but admire and like him. Most of all, because Spender has been so unsure of, and ambivalent toward, philosophy, aesthetics, religion, politics, and sexuality, and because he has equivocated and vacillated and, like all of us, has been tossed on the tide of historical events, his work provides a detailed portrait of a representative poet of the twentieth century.

Several people have helped me with this study. First of all, I am most grateful to Sir Stephen Spender for his kind cooperation and generous permission to quote from his work. I am also grateful to his brother Humphrey Spender, for further information on the Spender childhood and for the frontispiece photograph. At Syracuse University, Dr. Wendy Bousfield, Mrs. Mary Ellen O'Connell, and the incomparable interlibrary loan staff of Bird Library provided much-needed assistance.

Chronology

1909   Stephen Spender born 28 February in London, the third of four children of Edward Harold and Violet Hilda Schuster Spender.

1915   Family moves to Sheringham, Norfolk. Spender is enrolled in Miss Harcourt's School in East Runton.

1918   Is enrolled in Gresham's School, Holt, Norfolk.

1919   Family moves back to London.

1921   Mother dies. Spender is brought home to attend day school in Hampstead.

1925   Enrolls in University College School, London.

1926   Father dies. Children taken in by grandmother Hilda Schuster.

1928   Enters University College, Oxford, and meets W. H. Auden and Christopher Isherwood. *Nine Experiments* published.

1929   Coedits *Oxford Poetry: 1929* with Louis MacNeice.

1930   Leaves Oxford without degree. Follows Isherwood to Germany. *Twenty Poems* published.

1933   *Poems* published.

1934   *Vienna* published.

1935   *The Destructive Element* published.

1936   Marries Agnes Marie (Inez) Pearn. *The Burning Cactus* published.

1937   Joins British Communist party. Makes two trips to Spain. Returns disillusioned with communism. *Forward from Liberalism* published.

1938   *Trial of a Judge* is produced in London by Group Theatre and then published.

1939   Marriage dissolved. *The New Realism* and *The Still Centre* published.

1939–1941   Coedits *Horizon* magazine with Cyril Connolly and Peter Watson.

1940   *Selected Poems* and *The Backward Son* published.

1941   Marries Natasha Litvin.

1941–1944   Serves as fireman in London with National Fire Service.

1942   *Ruins and Visions* and *Life and the Poet* published.

1944   Is transferred to duty in the Foreign Office.

1945   In Occupied Germany with British Control Commission. Son Matthew born.

1946   With UNESCO in Paris. *European Witness* and *Poetry since 1939* published.

1947   *Poems of Dedication* published.

1947–1949   Makes first of several American sojourns.

1949   *The Edge of Being* published.

1950   Daughter Elizabeth born.

1951   *World within World* published.

1952   *Shelley* and *Learning Laughter* published.

1953   Serves as Elliston Professor of Poetry at the University of Cincinnati. *The Creative Element* published.

1953–1967   Coedits *Encounter* magazine with Irving Kristol and Melvin J. Lasky.

1955   *Collected Poems, 1928–1953* and *The Making of a Poem* published.

1958   *Engaged in Writing, and The Fool and the Princess* published.

1959   Serves as Beckman Professor at the University of California at Berkeley.

1962   Is named Commander of the British Empire.

1963   *The Struggle of the Modern* published.

1965–1966   Serves as consultant in poetry at Library of Congress.

1968   Witnesses student revolts at Columbia University, the Sorbonne, and the universities of Berlin and Prague.

1969   *The Year of the Young Rebels* and *The Generous Days* published.

1970–1977 Serves as professor of English at University College, London University.

1971 Is awarded Queen's Gold Medal for Poetry.

1974 *Love-Hate Relations* published.

1975 *T. S. Eliot* published.

1977 Is named Companion of Literature.

1978 *Recent Poems* and *The Thirties and After* published.

1979 Is made an honorary fellow of University College, Oxford.

1980 *Letters to Christopher, 1929–1939* published.

1982 Is knighted.

1985 *Collected Poems, 1928–1985* and *Journals, 1939–1983* published.

1988 *The Temple* published.

Chapter One
Generation of Hamlets: A Writer's Life

In historical, geopolitical, cultural, and sociological terms, the twentieth century started in 1914, when World War I ushered in the modern age. More than any other living British writer, Stephen Harold Spender is a child of the twentieth century. He was born in London on 28 February 1909 into an upper-middle-class English family at a time when Britain ruled a quarter of the earth's habitable surface, so that one might conclude, as did R. F. Delderfield, that even "God is an Englishman." When Spender was born the automobile, the airplane, and radio were in their infancy, and war was fought to a large extent on horseback, but he lived to see nuclear weaponry used, men walk on the moon, and the British Empire disintegrate.

Youth

Except for a few brief periods, Spender has maintained a residence all his life in the city of his birth, unlike so many other major modern writers who went into exile, self-imposed or forced, notably Mann and Joyce, Brecht and Brodsky, Pound and Beckett, and Auden and Eliot. Now this decent, liberal, sensitive, truthful, compassionate, loyal, self-deprecating old poet, still lean, tall, and handsome with white hair and blue eyes, remains very much an Englishman.

Spender's father, Harold, was a distinguished Liberal journalist and writer of books on Byron, political figures, and mountaineering. He ran unsuccessfully for Parliament from Bath as a United Liberal candidate. The senior Spender was the son of the well-known Victorian novelist Mrs. J. K. Spender and Dr. John Kent-Spender. He married the beautiful, sensitive, literarily talented, poetry writing Violet Schuster, 13 years his junior. Her parents were Ernest Schuster, a prominent barrister who was the son of a German Jewish banker, and

Hilda Weber Schuster, the intelligent, charitable, but eccentric daughter of the well-known Victorian physician Sir Herman Weber.

During World War I, in which Ernest and Hilda lost a son, this loyal British family was attacked by such anti-Semites as the Northcliffe Press, Hilaire Belloc, and G. K. Chesterton, who, as Stephen Spender says in his autobiography, *World within Worlds,* "interpreted the war as the defense of universal Catholicism against perfidious Germany and German-Jewry."[1] Spender did not learn of his Jewish ancestry until he was away at school. He then felt he understood why he had more in common with "the sensitive, rather soft, inquisitive interior Jewish boys, than with the aloof, hard, external English" (*WW,* 12), but he was somewhat repelled by his Jewish schoolmates' tendency toward self-hatred and self-pity, which seemed merely to increase their vulnerability. He was English by his own definition, yet his "feeling for the English was at times almost like being in love with an alien race" (*WW,* 12). In later biographical notes, Spender emphasized his "Jewishness"; rooting for the underdog is, after all, the "English" thing for a public-school, Oxford-educated, legacy-supported young man to do.

After the outbreak of World War I, Harold and Violet Spender moved to Sheringham, Norfolk, with their four children, Michael (born in 1907), Christine (1908), Stephen (1909), and Humphrey (1910). Stephen's nonage was not happy: his parents were puritanical, and Violet was often ill, sometimes hysterical, and given to frightening swings between love and hate, for she had lost her favorite brother in the war and grieved perpetually. Stephen found some solace in the garden, and he loved to walk alone in the woods and on the common near Sheringham. He early became a voracious reader and showed skill at painting, his avocation even now.

Stephen and his sister attended Miss Harcourt's School at nearby East Runton. Foreshadowing bisexual tendencies in maturity, at the age of seven Stephen had his first crush on a girl, but he also had homoerotic feelings for a boy with whom he wrestled. Stephen's first ambition was to be a naturalist like Charles Darwin, especially after a family trip to the Lake District. One day, as the war raged in Europe, a German zeppelin flew over the house, frightening all and foreshadowing the air raids the children would experience as adults in World War II (*WW,* 295). A love of science and a fear of war has remained with Spender all his life.

At nine Stephen decided to follow his older brother, Michael, to boarding school at the Old School House Preparatory School of

Gresham's School, Holt, because he wanted a school uniform like Michael's. He carried off to Gresham's one large trunk and one equally large box of caterpillars. Soon he was overcome by homesickness, but his appeals to home went unheeded as school was supposed to supply Stephen with the discipline his parents had failed to provide. The sensitive, unathletic child's encounters with a blustering, bullying headmaster and a cruel school gang proved so Dickensian an experience that Stephen dreamed of being crucified, but with ropes because he could not bear the imagined pain inflicted by nails. Fortunately, the terrorized and depressed boy was befriended by the music master, who comforted him with the assurance that he would be happy when he left the school to attend university. Indeed, the master prophesied that he would be "happier than most people" (*WW*, 302).

Spender was rescued from the shipwreck of his childhood by the family's return to London in 1919. Two years later, when Stephen was 12, his ailing mother failed to survive an operation. Harold Spender, never wholly successful as a father, suddenly turned into an overprotective mother hen to his brood, calling his children home to London from their respective schools, and Stephen was thereupon enrolled in a day school in Hampstead. Stephen's first encounter with the larger world of public events came in 1923: Harold Spender, then running for Parliament from Bath, brought Stephen and Humphrey down from London to help him campaign by riding around the streets of the city in a donkey cart with a placard around the animal's neck that read, "Vote for Daddy" (*WW*, 6). Harold lost.

Stephen Spender loved his father but could never grow close to him, because Harold seemed to employ ratiocination to maintain emotional distance from his children. In 1926 Harold died, like his wife, following an operation. Thus, Stephen was an orphan at 17. Supervision of the Spender children was assumed by their maternal grandmother, the remarkable Hilda Schuster. Stephen had, in fact, come under her strong influence two years before. She, unlike his father, understood the boy's taste for modern literature and painting. Indeed, when in 1925 Stephen enrolled in University College School, a day preparatory school in London, his father specifically forbade him from attending the theater and art galleries, but the subversive grandmother took him in secret.

Hilda Schuster was a woman of great sensibility, wide sympathies, and concern for the poor and the oppressed. During World War I she joined the Quakers. Although wealthy, she occupied only a single room in her large unheated apartment, saving on electricity by using tiny oil lamps, subsisting on stale bread and cheese, wearing simple black dresses, and giving all she possibly could to charity. She was, in short, an ascetic aesthete. Grandmother Schuster and Stephen's paternal uncle, the Liberal journalist J. A. Spender, encouraged him in his early desire to become a poet. The uncle introduced Stephen to the poet Frank Kendon, who so impressed the boy that he determined to make poetry his life work and live in the country of the imagination.

Mrs. Schuster sent Stephen to Nantes to live with a Protestant minister and learn French prior to going up to Oxford. There he was deeply attracted to a beautiful English lad, also 18. The relationship came close to a sexual fulfillment, but fear prevented it. Class restrictions, inhibitions, puritanical relatives, and the English school system had conspired to keep the young man from any opportunity to meet, and to be sexually attracted to, young women. The result for Spender and for many young men of his background was an initial predilection for the love that was available: same-sex love. Spender deplores labels such as "homosexual" and "heterosexual," and argues on historical lines for bisexuality, although admitting that a normal sexual relationship is one between man and woman. Still, a "relationship of the highest understanding can be between two people of the same sex" (WW, 61). That relationship, of course, can exist with or without physical consummation.

Innocent, sexually confused, shy, intensely self-conscious, guilt-laden, undisciplined, naive, but very idealistic, Spender found himself entrained for Oxford, sure of only one thing: he would be a poet. Already he had acquired a small hand press and published an edition of 18 copies of *Nine Experiments* (1928) for friends and relatives.

Early Manhood

Oxford disappointed Spender. Although he had had a privileged early education, he had not attended the truly posh schools like Eton and Harrow, and he was snubbed by those who had. His interest in poetry, painting, and music and a studied eccentricity in dress made him seem very strange indeed. Desperate for friendship, he forced himself on another undergraduate and tried to acquire an interest in his friend's athleticism. They made a walking tour, but the relationship failed. Spender learned he could not find himself in the eyes or the esteem of another. He turned to voracious reading: Shakespeare, the Elizabethans, the Romantic poets, and the moderns. He "covered reams of paper with ungrammatical incoherent sentences which I imagined to resemble the style of James Joyce in *Ulysses*" (*WW*, 35).

Fortunately, Stephen's brother Michael, ahead of him at Oxford, introduced him to a school friend whose poetry Stephen admired: W. H. Auden. By means of his wit, dominating intelligence, and self-confidence, Auden had already established himself with his Oxford contemporaries as their leader in literary taste. Auden did not converse; he lectured and everyone else listened. Young Spender, who printed a collection of Auden's poems on his small press, became his disciple in all ways, including sex.[2] Auden also introduced Spender to the beautiful Christopher Isherwood, his favorite male lover. Isherwood, calling Spender "Stephen Savage" in his autobiographical *Lions and Shadows*, notes that the younger writer "was the slave of his friends," and in reference to Spender's idealism, said, "You know why he's so tall? He's trying to reach heaven."[3]

Auden was the major influence on the early development of Spender the poet. Before Auden, Spender "thought that poetry should create a special world" by shutting out the real world. Under Auden's tutelage Spender realized "how essential it was to make reality the vital material of poetic creation."[4] No longer did he believe, as Shelley had, that "poets are the unacknowledged legislators of the world." The stuff of modern poetry had to be the unpoetic-seeming things around him, even the mundane gasworks on the beautiful path on which the two young poets strolled along Oxford's canal. The anomoly of a Creation both beautiful and ugly, sordid and sublime, provided a numen for a decade or more of poetry.

Spender saw some of the darker realities of his day and culture, and he reveled in them during one summer vacation in Berlin, where Isherwood was living his *Berlin Stories*. Spender was captivated by the blazing vitality and unmitigated decadence of life in Weimar Germany.

When Spender returned to Oxford after his first summer vacation, Auden had graduated, and the younger poet enlarged his circle of friends to include poets like Louis MacNeice and Bernard Spencer. With MacNeice he coedited the 1929 issue of the annual *Oxford Poetry*. Each contributed four pieces to the publication. MacNeice's description of Spender at Oxford is cogent and charming: "Spender was the nearest to the popular romantic conception of a poet—a towering angel not quite sure if he was fallen, thinking of himself as the poet always, moving in his own limelight. He was already taking upon himself the travail of the world, undergoing a chronic couvade. Redeeming the world by introspection. Physically clumsy, he combined with the glamour of the born martyr the charm of some great shaggy animal and—a saving grace in my eyes—you always could make him giggle."[5]

At this time Spender's political views, like his aesthetics, came to maturity, which may account for why he approached politics with a poet's sensibility and wrote poetry with a committed politician's concern for society. It is the tension between these aspects of the man that gives force to Spender's early, great poetry. Moved by the gentle humanitarianism of Grandmother Schuster, Spender saw all too clearly the arrogance and frivolity of the wealthier students at Oxford and Cambridge, the deplorable conditions of the working class, the vast army of unemployed in the Great Depression, and the injustice of the class system. With a sense of guilt at having profited by being born to a privileged class, Spender embraced socialism as the answer to society's grave ills.

In 1930, at the end of his second year at Oxford, Spender dropped out of the university and never earned a degree. (Almost fifty years later, University College would make him an honorary fellow.) But at 21 he had to follow his new star, Isherwood, to Germany again. On a walk through Berlin with a friend of Isherwood's called Chalmers in *Lion and Shadows*, Spender was convinced that his conscience could only be assuaged by embracing Marxism. William York Tyndall notes that guilt ridden upper-middle-class British liberals were drawn to the Communist party because as "an antidote to dying capitalism that party offered a classless society."[6] But more than anything else, it was the threat of fascism and the inability of Western capitalist states to contain that menace that pushed Spender into the arms of the far Left. He was certainly not alone in his generation. Many young people were disappointed with capitalist democracy. Communism appeared to offer greater justice for the masses, and only communism seemed ready to oppose fascism.

In 1930, Blackwell, a commercial publisher, issued Spender's *Twenty Poems* in a limited edition. Publication brought him the acquaintance of the Bloomsbury Group and the patronage of Harold Nicolson and Virginia Woolf, who nevertheless, in "A Letter to a Young Poet" (1932) criticized Spender, Auden, and C. Day Lewis for impatience and preoccupation with external social problems and the unrealistic desire to see justice prevail in the real world. Their poems, she said, are written "for the eye of a severe and intelligent public," but should have been written for their own eyes. Furthermore, "they have been exposed to the fierce

light of publicity while they were too young to stand the strain."[7]
Thus, out of jealousy Woolf argues for and against a Romantic strategy:
write only for yourself but wait until after 30 to publish.

At this time Spender also met T. S. Eliot, who quickly became a
major influence on the young poet's subsequent work in the 1930s and
remained a lifelong friend. In 1933 Faber and Faber, where Eliot
worked as an editor, began to publish Spender after the *New Signatures*
(1932) anthology of Michael Roberts featured the young generation of
socially conscious writers, but it was when Spender's poetry began to
appear in such leading periodicals as the *New Statesman,* the *Listener,*
Adelphi, and *Twentieth Century* that it was clear he had made a break-
through. He was also being translated into German and French. Faber
and Faber's publication of *Poems* (1933) thrust the 24-year-old poet into
the first rank of contemporary poets. He had ignored Woolf's advice
with a vengeance. Spender was now being compared to another handsome young radical poet who also had come down from Oxford: Shelley.

With Auden's *Poems* (1930), Day Lewis's *From Feathers to Iron* (1931)
and Spender's *Poems,* the radical poetry movement of the 1930s was
under way. Variously called "the Oxford Group," "the Auden Group,"
"the Pylon Poets," and "the New Signatures," the members of the
movement—notably Auden, Spender, Day Lewis, and MacNeice—
had come of age. Spender later called them the "Divided Generation of
Hamlets who found the world out of joint and failed to set it right"
(*WW,* 83). They, including many lesser contemporaries like John Lehmann, William Empson, Julian Bell, and David Gascoyne, were almost
all socialists or communists, sons of the upper middle class or upper
class, recipients of exclusive private educations, admirers of Eliot,
Pound, and Yeats, frequently bisexual or homosexual, and generally
misogynistic. As they took over the organs of literature, their disdain
for women did much harm, so that, for example, a protofeminist poet
from the lower middle class like Stevie Smith had small chance of
breaking the hold of the truculent cabal.[8]

Meanwhile, Spender considered marriage as an antidote to his diffi-
dence and personal loneliness, but instead he employed as a secretary a
young man with whom he was soon sexually involved and to whom he
addressed love poems and dedicated books. In *World within World* (159)
Spender calls him Jimmy Younger, but in *Journals, 1939–1983* he
reveals that his lover was T. A. R. (Tony) Hyndman.[9] In 1923 they
traveled through Europe together, living for the most part on Spender's
inheritance and enjoying an otiose existence even as Spender lamented

the poverty and deprivation he saw throughout Europe, particularly in Austria and Germany. They quarreled frequently, and Spender eventually realized that he could not be happy living with a man. He needed love and commitment for and from a woman. Wholeness in life, he decided, could only come from heterosexual love (*WW*, 168–69).

Vienna, Spender's long poem about Engelbert Dollfuss's brutal suppression of the Austrian Socialist rebellion in the capital during February 1934, was published later that year. Also that year, while still involved with Hyndman, Spender began an affair with the beautiful Elizabeth ————, a 29-year-old American double divorcee with a child. She was studying medicine and psychology in Vienna. They moved into her apartment while Hyndman was in the hospital having his appendix out. Stephen, ever the loyal friend, could not abandon Tony, even though he was in love with Elizabeth. Young and with limited heterosexual experience, he did not satisfy her (*WW*, 182). Frustrated by Spender's ambivalence, Elizabeth wavered. They separated. Stephen returned to London, ostensibly for a visit, and Elizabeth quickly found a man with whom she could be happy. When Spender returned to Vienna, she introduced him to her fiancé and all three became friends.

Spender had participated with her in the Socialist cells, finding himself drawn closer to the far Left. He began to write *Forward from Liberalism*, published in 1937, in which Spender argues that liberals must support the only "ism" that was fighting fascism and, for the long term, reconcile communist social justice and fairness for all segments of society with liberals' special regard for social freedom. This was the only time in Spender's long life when he accorded social justice precedence over individual freedom.

Spender's first and most important work of criticism, *The Destructive Element*, was published in 1935, establishing his credentials as a literary critic. In it he argues that Henry James initiated the modernist movement and that his successors are Yeats, Eliot, and D. H. Lawrence.

Spender was in Vienna in July 1936 when he learned of the outbreak of the Spanish Civil War. He returned to London feeling that his personal life was a failure, and he resolved to break with Hyndman. *The Burning Cactus* (1936), a collection of his stories, had just been published, and so he now had credibility and reputation as a fiction writer as well as a poet and a critic. *Forward from Liberalism* would soon extend his range to political theory. Invited to Oxford to speak on behalf of aid to Spain, he met a very progressive, fetching, fair-haired girl, a student of Spanish literature and, like Spender, a supporter of the Republican cause. Agnes Marie (Inez) Pearn and Stephen Spender quickly became engaged and were married within three weeks of their first meeting. They wed in Hilda Schuster's Kensington flat, with Auden and Isherwood in attendance. Thereupon, Hyndman discreetly joined the International Brigade and left Britain to soldier in Spain.

Unfortunately, Inez and Stephen soon found that they hardly knew each other. Immaturity and a concern for Spain were all they had in common. They came to realize that they were not a good match.

When *Forward from Liberalism* appeared, the secretary of the British Communist party, Harry Pollitt, asked Spender to help the beleaguered Spanish Republic by fighting the fascist Nationalists and, if necessary, dying for liberty, like a twentieth-century Byron. Spender refused, for he was, and is, a pacifist. Pollitt then asked him to write an article for the communist *Daily Worker* expressing his views on the need for liberals to move left in the struggle with fascism; he also asked Spender to join the Communist party. Spender agreed to do both. He received a party membership card but never was asked to pay dues; within a year, he was disillusioned with communism and the party.

Spender was again asked to go to Spain, not to fight this time but to investigate for the *Daily Worker* the fate of the crew of a Russian ship sunk by the Italians while carrying arms for the Spanish Republic. By this time Hyndman had proved to be a poor soldier, weak and disobedient. After his first battle experience his value as a fighter was nugatory, and he was soon in trouble for attempted desertion. Spender felt responsible for this, believing that Hyndman had become a communist under his influence and never would have gone to Spain but for the broken relationship with the poet. Spender used the opportunity of his assignment in Spain to get Hyndman transferred to noncombatant duty, although Hyndman begged Spender to get him out of the International Brigade, which at first his friend was unwilling and unable to do. On a second trip to Spain, Spender did manage to arrange for Hyndman's discharge and repatriation to Britain, thus saving his life.

In Madrid on his second visit, as a writer representing Great Britain, Spender become completely disenchanted with communism. The communist literati bickered, jostled for privileges, and lied. They reported Nationalist atrocities but refused to acknowledge those committed by the Left. Communist officers were more concerned with indoctrination than with victory, and continually purged those volunteers who did not slavishly adhere to the party line. For Spender the campaign was not an exercise in idealism but Machiavellian political opportunism and purposive hypocrisy.

Spender met Ernest Hemingway in Spain, "a hairy-handed giant. . . . He seemed at first to be acting the part of a Hemingway hero" (*WW*, 208). They became friends however, although Hemingway was convinced that Spender was "too squeemish." A few months before, in London, Graham Greene had met Spender for the first time and pronounced him "one as having too much of the milk of human kindness. A little soft."[10] Sensitive people first meeting Spender often commented on his gentleness. Later they would come to realize the strength of his commitment to art and humanitarianism. Spender also met and became friends with André Malraux in Spain. Both writers shared a liberal individualism and opposed lockstep communism. Together they battled hard-line, brainwashed writers and policians, and struggled for truth, integrity, and respect for the individual.

Back in England, never to return to embattled Spain, Stephen and Inez rented a cottage on the Kentish coast. *Trial of a Judge,* a five-act verse tragedy about the dilemma of a liberal judge torn between ideologies, which Spender wrote for Rupert Doone's Group Theatre, opened in London on 18 March 1938, to positive reviews.

By this time Spender's marriage was going badly. Seeking help, he turned to psychoanalysis, but found Freud as disappointing as Marx. A return to serious painting helped relieve his mental anguish and tension, as did the writing of a series of poems stemming from his experiences in Spain. Inez had tolerated Stephen's obsession with antifascism, his trips to Spain, the importance of his writer friends in his life, and even his concern for Hyndman, but in the summer of 1939 she fell in love with, and left Spender for, the poet and sociologist Charles Madge (*J*, 21). Divorce ensued. Spender was badly hurt, but his personal suffering was overshadowed by the fall of the Spanish Republic and the complete failure of all the efforts the Left had made to prevent a total European war. The Hitler-Stalin Non-Agression Pact finished communism for most of the rest of the British intellectual Left. On 1 September 1939 the Germans invaded Poland. Two days later, Great Britain was at war.

War and Maturity

The Still Centre, which appeared in 1939, is a collection of poems that marks a turning point in Spender's career. It shows that Spender had shifted some of his literary allegiance away from T. S. Eliot and had come under the influence of Wilfred Owen and, to a lesser extent, D. H. Lawrence. *The Still Centre* evidences the poet's turn away from political verse to personal and private poetry. As to Auden's influence, although Spender still employed his mentor's sudden, unexpected shifts of focus, he nevertheless had passed the crisis in what Harold Bloom calls "the anxiety of influence."

For almost two years, from late 1939 to 1941, Spender coedited *Horizon* magazine with Cyril Connolly and Peter Watson, working out of Spender's flat in Bloomsbury, where he was living alone, until they evacuated to Devonshire, where he continued to work on the magazine and also taught school for one term. Despite a world in chaos and flame, Spender's creative life endured and flourished, evidenced by *Selected Poems* and the autobiographical novel *The Backward Son,* both published in 1940.

In 1941 Spender returned to London, where he was called up for military service but failed the physical. He joined the National Fire Service. Although still a strong pacifist, he could save lives and help the war effort against the Nazis as a fireman during the fierce air raids that were immolating London. One fire isolated Spender in a blazing building and nearly ended his life. Still, Spender was lucky in that the Blitz stopped shortly after he began fire-fighting duties, and the buzz bombs started dropping two days after he left the Fire Service in 1944 to take up duties with the Foreign Office.

Spender's acceptance of a job that was often as dangerous as combat contrasts sharply with actions of Auden and Isherwood, who had emigrated to America in January 1939 and remained there during the war, for which they were much criticized. As to other radical poets, Mac-Neice volunteered for the Royal Navy, but was rejected because of poor eyesight and became a London fire watcher, and Day Lewis served in the Ministry of Information in London.

On 9 April 1941, Spender married the concert pianist Natasha Litvin, beginning a long and happy relationship. For a while they lived in an attic flat in Mansfield Gardens, Hampstead, a few doors from where Sigmund Freud had lived during his brief London sojourn and his daughter and disciple, Anna, now ran a nursery for child victims of the war.

In 1942, Spender's poetry collection *Ruins and Visions* was published, both featuring and terminating his poetry of the Proletarian Decade. Complementing it is *Life and the Poet* (1942), which attacks the attempts to make poetry serve causes in a Platonic, functional, subjective mode and argues that poetry must take sides only with life. In 1949 Spender would fully confess his disillusionment with communism and its regimentation of artists, in a salient essay contributed to Richard Crossman's landmark collection of essays, *The God That Failed*. It was as pertinent in 1989 as it had been in 1949.

The year 1945 brought Spender great personal joy and sorrow. March saw the birth of the Spenders' first child, Matthew, during one of the worst night attacks of the V2 rockets. (Neighbor Anna Freud taught Natasha child care.) But on Christmas Day, Spender's sister-in-law Margaret Spender, to whom he had been very close, died of cancer after great suffering, having endured with much courage. Deeply moved, Spender commemorated the brave woman in a six-part poem, "Elegy for Margaret."

With the end of the war in Europe, Spender was sent to occupied Germany to work with the British Control Commission, and in *Citizens in War—and After* (1945) Spender discusses and illustrates the new roles civilian populations must play in wartime. In 1946 Spender was working for UNESCO in Paris, but soon resigned when the General Assembly failed to reelect Julian Huxley as general secretary of UNESCO because of the machinations of an American delegation under the influence of early McCarthyism.

Paradoxically, as Spender became more of a public person, his poetry grew more personal and consequently less intense and less universal. Spender began to give more time to criticism and social history than to poetry, though his interest in writing poetry did not lessen. *European Witness* (1946) documents Spender's extensive travel and many conversations in postwar Germany, trying to circumscribe, comprehend, and explain the paresis in German intellectual and imaginative life. He also began to apply his considerable critical skills to contemporary British poetry with *Poetry since 1939* (1946). *Poems of Dedication* (1947), which includes the Margaret poems, are almost entirely introspective and personal, exploring themes of birth, death, love and separation, and philosophy.

In 1947, Spender began his lifelong, happy, and profitable relationship with the United States, where to this day he enjoys a literary regard equal to or surpassing his British reputation. Sarah Lawrence College convinced him to join Mary McCarthy, Horace Gregory, Randall Jarrell, Robert Fitzgerald, and Joseph Campbell on its star-studded faculty for an academic year. Over the next 38 years Spender and his family would frequently reside up to six months a year at American universities, including the University of Cincinnati, the University of California at Berkeley, Northwestern University, the University of Connecticut, the University of Florida at Gainesville, Cornell College and Grinnell College in Iowa, Vanderbilt University, the University of Louisville, and Emory University.

With the publication of the collection *The Edge of Being* (1949), Spender began to revise his earlier poetry, sometimes superficially and sometimes radically, but usually infelicitously. In 1950 the Spenders' second and last child, Elizabeth, was born. Spender's excellent autobiography of his life to age 40, *World within World*, on which he had worked for five years, was published to very favorable reviews, and was immediately recognized as the most significant account of the development of the thirties poets. It remains one of the most frequently quoted autobiographies of the period, for Spender's "is the kind of personality made for autobiography, and *World within World* is an absorbing and considerable book, an important, eloquent apologia."[11]

In 1953 Spender's entry into the United States was contested by proponents of then-rampant McCarthyism, but conservative Senator Robert Taft interceded on his behalf, and Spender had no further trouble with the American government. That year, Spender's second most important critical work, *The Creative Element*, appeared. In it Spender attempts to define creativity and concludes that the main impulse of the modern moment is individual vision.

At this time Spender also embarked upon an enterprise that would begin as one of his most successful but end in a debacle. Along with Irving Kristol and Melvin J. Lasky he founded and edited one of the most distinguished and widely read literary and political journals of midcentury, *Encounter*, which was sponsored by the Congress for Cultural Freedom. Much later, Frank Kermode joined the staff. *Encounter* was liberal and anticommunist. Funding came through the Farfield Foundation. In fact, the foundation was a channel for Central Intelligence Agency (CIA) funds. Spender knew nothing of this until 1967, for he had been purposely deceived. When the truth was made public, he immediately resigned. The incident not only caused Spender deep embarrassment but subjected him to skepticism and even ridicule. "The *Encounter* association and divorce only reinforced the common image of the faded pink whose left hand was so ignorant of the right hand's doings that it could work for ten years against its own real interests."[12] In its stupidity the CIA destroyed a superb journal and betrayed true Anglo-American values of openness and nongovernmental interference in intellectual and artistic activities.

Collected Poems, 1928–1953 (1955) is the high-water mark of Spender's popularity and critical reception; it reminded the reading public of his many well-crafted, emotionally moving poems. The year 1955 also saw the publication of *The Making of a Poem,* a collection of essays that highlights poetry's dependence on the poet's memory and argues that nothing can be imagined that is unrelated to experience. Spender's talents as a writer of fiction were displayed in the novellas *Engaged in Writing, and the Fool and the Princess,* published jointly in book form in 1958.

The Elder Statesman

Stephen Spender was now known the world over. He was lecturing and teaching throughout North America. He attended PEN conferences with other renowned writers in the capitals of Europe and Asia and was welcomed as an honored guest in the Soviet Union, India, China, Japan, and elsewhere. Honors began to accrue: Spender became a Commander of the British Empire in 1962, and in 1965, he was appointed consultant in poetry for the Library of Congress. In 1970 Spender obtained his only British academic appointment, but it was a most distinguished one: professor of English at University College, London University. He taught there until 1977, when he went on the academic road again to America. He received the Queen's Gold Medal for Poetry from Queen Elizabeth II in 1971.

In 1960 the Spenders, by then relatively affluent, bought an old farmhouse in the south of France as a second residence and have since lived there three months out of every year. In September 1961 Spender's translation-adaption of Friedrich von Schiller's *Maria Stuart* was produced by the Old Vic Company at the Edinburgh Festival and was so well received that the play was transferred to London for a long run, with the distinguished actress Irene Worth as the Scottish queen. Spender's next work was his third major piece of literary criticism, *The Struggle of the Modern* (1963), an evaluation of the modernist moment long after it had passed.

If the *Encounter* affair of 1967 depressed Spender, it did not do so for long, because he was caught up in the revolutionary events of 1968. Once again world tragedy overshadowed, and distracted him from, his personal difficulties. The nations of the West had not known such internal trauma since the Central and Eastern European revolutions of 1917–19, and because almost all of those in revolt were students, the events of 1968 can best be compared to the upheavals of 1848, the fateful year that saw the rise both of Marxism and fierce reactionaryism. Spender's time-muted radicalism again found its voice, and he chose to become the Thucydides of the Parnassian War. He climbed through a window into the office of the president of Columbia University to debate with and for students. He flew to Paris and closely observed "the very stylized student re-enactment of past revolutions" (*J*, 258). He was briefly trapped by the violence in Paris, but eventually made his way to Berlin and then to Prague, where he applauded the students of Charles University, who were fighting for the school's long tradition of intellectual freedom. Back at Mas St Jérôme, his French residence, in the summer of 1968, Spender listened to the radio tolling the painful news, hour by hour, of the Red Army's occupation of Prague. *The Year of the Young Rebels* (1969) resulted from Spender's concern for, and involvement in, the struggle of the students.

During the 1960s, young poets and critics came down hard on the "anchronistic" thirties poet, but Spender did not go truffle-sniffing to find enemies in every book and article. If Spender was Shelley grown old, his spirit remained as free and as generous as Ariel's. Although Spender was writing and publishing less poetry than he had in earlier decades, he had by no means abandoned Euterpe: *The Generous Days,* a slim volume of mostly elegiac verse, appeared in 1969. Although few in number, the poems therein and in the even briefer *Recent Poems* (1978) indicate a resurgence in poetic vitality. The Spender canon reveals a pattern frequently found in the works of poets, wherein the poet seems to lose interest in his craft during middle age but returns to it with some power in old age.

Always concerned with political and artistic freedom, Spender co-founded the *Index on Censorship,* a magazine dedicated to making the international public aware of the suppression of expression anywhere it exists; he continues to serve on the editorial board. *Love-Hate Relations* (1974), Spender's study of Anglo-American sensibilities, was followed by *T. S. Eliot* (1975), an appreciation of his mentor. *The Thirties and After* (1978) encapsulates the political and social history of the 1930s through the 1970s in a series of essays, reminiscences, journal entries, and commentaries. Spender also took the opportunity to explain the *Encounter* episode in detail.

In 1977, Spender was made a Companion of Literature by the Royal

Society of Literature, of which he was already a fellow. Two years later, Oxford recognized the contributions of a notable dropout when Spender's old college, University College, elected him an honorary fellow.

Spender suffered a setback in 1980 when he fell on a rain-slickened pavement outside the Finchley Road station. He tore the ligaments in both knees and was hospitalized for months. Natasha took him, limping and in pain, to Louisville, Kentucky, to fulfill a teaching engagement at the university. The charming, pixilated Spender remarks that falling in 1980 was most fortuitous because it was the Year of the Disabled and "the university was full of equipment recently installed to deal with such a case as mine" (*J*, 395). While he was in America, Spender's 1929–39 correspondence with Isherwood was published: *Letters to Christopher* (1980). Adjusting easily and kindly to the shifting rhythms of friendship, Spender maintained all his youthful relationships insofar as life, age, and time permitted.

In 1981 he was off to China with the artist David Hockney, an adventurous trip that resulted in *China Diary* (1982). By this point in his life, the onetime Communist had reached such a degree of acceptance, recognition, and respectability that the British government, in the name of Queen Elizabeth, offered him a knighthood in 1982, and he accepted.

For Sir Stephen, 1985 was an annus mirabilis for it witnessed the publication of *Collected Poems, 1928–1985* and *Journals, 1939–1983* and a performance of his adaptation of the *Oedipus* trilogy. In 1988 Spender revised and published for the first time an autobiographical novel written some 55 years earlier, *The Temple*, concerned with a handsome young Englishman's appreciation of the male body during the Weimar era in Germany. The story mixes an elated sense of liberated homosexualty with a febrile excitement induced by the terrifying rise of Nazism and the lure of communism. Spender's revision of the novel entailed a change of setting from the effervescent Germany of 1929 to the more somber and fearful Germany of 1932, the year before Hitler's assumption of the chancellorship.

Spender among the Moderns

Unlike their younger counterparts, today's leading British and Irish poets in their middle and later years—Charles Tomlinson, Ted Hughes, and Seamus Heaney among them—all assimilated modernism from their earliest education onward. The cultural common denominator—an accepted canon—is now only spottily taught in Britain, Ireland, and North America and is therefore less fundamental and formative. In the essay "Young Poets in the 1970s," Blake Morrison points out that in his secondary education in the England of the 1960s capable teachers made sure he became familiar with Eliot's "Prufrock," *The Waste Land,* and *The Cocktail Party;* Joyce's *Dubliners, Portrait of the Artist,* and *Ulysses;* Lawrence's *Sons and Lovers* and *Lady Chatterley's Lover;* Hardy's *Poems of 1912–13;* Sean O'Casey's *The Silver Tassie;* Wilfred Owen's *Collected Poems;* Beckett's *Waiting for Godot* and *Endgame;* "plus bits of Yeats, Sassoon, Rosenberg, Graves, Auden, Spender and Dylan Thomas."[13]

Arguably, these were the literary giants of the century. In poetry the Yeats-Eliot-Auden-Spender axis was the grand architectonic of twentieth-century British poetry. Morrison and his schoolmates were the last recipients of the undiluted canon of modernism, of which Spender was a part.

Stephen Spender's literary output is enormous, for he has had to live by his words, doing book reviewing, art criticism, and journalism as well as poetry. Perusing his bibliography in the 1970s, he defined his canon as that which he thought best represented him: "fifty poems, a handful of stories, *World within World, Trial of a Judge* (an unsatisfying but genuinely felt work), a few essays, such as the one called 'The Making of a Poem,' some translations. This already seems quite a list."[14] Even Spender could feel overwhelmed by the volume of his output.

They are all gone now except for him. The giants. And the thirties poets—those brilliant, precocious, privileged, troubled, radical, conscience-stricken, snobbish, handsome Oxford poets. The great bright hope of British poetry right before World War II. The gang their reactionary enemy the poet Roy Campbell called "MacSpaunday." MacNeice died in 1963, Day Lewis in 1972, and Auden in 1973. Christopher Isherwood of Cambridge, who was forever linked with them, died in 1986.

Cynthia Ozick, lamenting what postmodern writers have lost, something the moderns like Spender had, said that a later generation will "go on missing forever . . . that golden cape of youth, the power and prestige of high art."[15] Stephen Spender could, and can still, revel in that power.

Chapter Two
A Thirties Poet: Early Verse

Tagged "the Auden Group," "the Oxford Poets," "the Pylon Poets," and other sobriquets, W. H. Auden, Stephen Spender, and C. Day Lewis were the leaders—and in critical opinion the only notable members—of a group of politically radical poets concerned with humanity and society and the dilemma of the seemingly unavoidable choice between necessity and freedom. They sought a truer vision of human existence. "They held that man was a product of his environment, that to change him the environment had to be transformed."[1] Michael Roberts, in his preface to *New Signatures* (1932), describes the rebellion of the new poets against the long tradition of introspective and esoteric poetry.[2] The group disintegrated with the advent of World War II, when the Marxist beliefs that bound them to each other were found wanting. Spender became the first to fall away.

The major characteristic of Spender's poetry is a constant tension between an engagement with the objective world outside—the salient mark of the thirties poets—and the need for his soaring spirit to rise above the mundane considerations of the workaday world. The result was "the fragmentation of self."[3] Forever in Spender's favor is his perpetual belief that poetry is a human gesture. As a poet emerging between the two great wars of this sad century, he naturally took as his subjects fear and death, love and war, inhibition and weakness, but always Spender had his own private drama to play out before his readers—"a struggle to adapt his individualism to his social views, and a struggle to understand and perfect his individuality."[4]

Auden was Spender's leader, mentor, and benign Svengali. Day Lewis and MacNeice were coequals with Spender in a "gang of four." In retrospect, the members of the group appear more different than alike, and at least one critic now believes that "Spender" was . . . Auden's superior as a poet."[5]

Nine Experiments

Spender's juvenalia is relatively impressive. During the summer vacation of 1928, Spender obtained a small hand-operated printing press and published his *Nine Experiments: Being Poems Written at the Age of Eighteen*. Exactly eighteen hand-numbered copies were issued. Spender soon became dissatisfied with his venture, tore up the loose sheets, and tried to retrieve and destroy the copies he had distributed. However, in 1964 he allowed a facsimile edition to be published by the Elliston Poetry Foundation at the University of Cincinnati.

The nine poems encompass a variety of subjects, but the major theme of *Nine Experiments* is the redeeming power of love in relation to the social problems of humankind. From the precocious beginning, Spender was intent on using and transforming much of the seemingly nonpoetic material of life in an industrial society. The noisy, malodorous, machine-run world of technology must be reconciled with the inherent beauty and majesty of the natural world.

In "Come, Let Us Praise the Gasworks!" Spender challenges the commonplace and shows his desire to explore new realms of experience, even (hypothetically of course) hard manual labor, surely a romantic trait:

> And man, the grimmest, starkest
> Of all those intimate machines; the harshest
> Grate grate [sic]. I'd love
> In an archaically perfect mechanic to move
> With clock-work limbs.[6]

The gasworks, providers of energy, are vital to an industrial society with a huge population. Louis Untermeyer very quickly perceived that "while the belated Georgians were still invoking literary laverocks, lonely lambs, and traditionally deathless nightingales, Spender was hailing the advent of another order and writing such poems as 'Come, Let Us Praise the Gasworks.' "[7]

> Walking beside a stenchy black canal,
> Regarding skies obtusely animal,
> Contemplating rubbish heaps, and smoke,
> And tumid furnaces, obediently at work.
> (*NE*, 14)

In trying to circumscribe the effects of poverty, "Appeal" anticipates Spender's later sympathies. It opens thus: "The voices of the poor, like birds / That thud against a sullen pane, / Have worn my heart" (*NE*, 8). However, the persona finds himself growing indifferent to the victims of society because their suffering is not as great as his grief for an unrequited love: "*It is upon your heart, your heart / That knows not charity*" (*NE*, 8).

The opening poem of *Nine Experiments,* "Invocation," self-consciously echoes Shelley's "Ode to the West Wind": "Blow for ever in my head! / And ever let the violins, tempest-sworn, / Lash out their hurricane" (*NE*, 7). Fortunately, Spender never again would mix a metaphorical stew of violins and a hurricane.

Exploring the world of nature, "Evening on the Lake—(dolce)" pulsates with romantic vocabulary and imagery:

> Beauty cometh: See how gently
> Graven in the Water, play
> The lazy whorls, which, Whirl absently
> Round the prow, and Glide away.
>
> (*NE*, 17)

The almost 19-year-old poet sees himself, as teenagers are wont to do, as sophisticated and world-weary in "Ovation for Spring":

> The nineteenth time, from bough to bough
> I see the mocking fires of spring;
> And twice I've rhymed the name with "king,"
> But I am grown more *blasé* now.
>
> (*NE*, 19)

The beauty of spring has lost its romantic hold on the persona. "The world is too much with him." Spring

> cannot stir me with her sound,
> Her light no longer makes me burn:
> I only see earth wake, and turn
> Again in penitential round.
>
> (*NE*, 19)

In *Nine Experiments,* Spender initiates his iterative light imagery with the related sun and eye references. Also, he begins to allude to glass and windowpanes as dividers of realities. As a group, these first poems show the promise of a young, intelligent, sensitive, impassioned poet striving to go beyond seeing to find a perspective into a personal realm of feeling, a poet at his best when working with the common idiom.

"Invocation," "Epistle," "I must repress," "Boiling the desperate cof-
fee," "From 'The Enshrinement of the Ideal,' Part iv," "Made Sober,"
and "The Farewell" were all deemed forgettable by Spender and critics
and never anthologized or collected.

Twenty Poems

The first critical attention to Spender's poetry was provoked by
Twenty Poems of 1930 (*WW*, 131). The collection proved much more
durable than *Nine Experiments*. Fourteen of the pieces appear in *Poems*
(1933), 13 in the slightly revised 1934 edition, and the 14 of the 1933
volume in *Collected Poems* (1955).

In these poems the Spenderian conflict between his basic romanti-
cism and his growing understanding of the harsh realities of society
grows more evident. The true poet must be affected by the climate of
his age. G. S. Fraser notes, "There is a deep inherited wish in Mr
Spender to yield to the romantic afflatus; there is also a strong contemporary impulse to question it and check it."[8] It is this duality, this tense
entwining of thesis and antithesis, that provides the foundation for the
earlier and greater part of the Spender canon.

In *Twenty Poems,* Spender begins to evince an individual style and
work out the concept of the poem not only as statement but as act.
Thus, there is a prescient openness in the verse. A distinct voice begins
to emerge from the center of self.

The initial poem in *Twenty Poems* is so significant a statement for
Spender that he used a phrase from it 20 years later as the title for the
volume of poems *The Edge of Being* (1949). The poem "At the Edge of
Being" begins, "Never being, but always at the edge of Being." The
persona has decided to separate himself from full participation in life.
He moves his lips for tasting and his hands for touching but can never
get nearer to life than allowed by sensory limitations:

> Though the Spirit lean outward for seeing.
> Observing rose, gold, eyes, an admired landscape.
> My senses record the act of wishing
> Wishing to be
> Rose, gold, landscape or another—
> Claiming fulfilment in the act of loving.[9]

As happens often in the Spender canon, the self is split: part is in the
world of the will and part remains in what Spender would later call "the

still centre." The spirit in the center can only lean out and touch the
world. Yet "the act of loving" ("the fact of loving" in later versions),
desirable as it is, tempts the persona toward oneness, the convergence
of world and self. The poet, however, prefers the safety of the edge,
where his fragile art is inviolable.

One series of personal verses in *Twenty Poems* is called the "Marston
Poems," four of which were published in *Oxford Poetry* (1929) and six of
which were reprinted in *Poems* (1933). They relate to Spender's infatua-
tion with a fellow undergraduate at Oxford, an athletic but sensitive
young man. The one-sided relationship was heartbreakingly frustrating
(*WW,* 64–67): "Rushing in room and door flung wide, I knew. / On
empty walls, book-carcases, blank chairs / All splintered in my head
and cried for you" (*TP,* 7). "Marston" did not reciprocate Spender's
passion, but nevertheless treated his young admirer politely, a quality
that further endeared him to the poet. The "Marston Poems" com-
mence with "Discovered in Mid-Ocean," in which the persona allevi-
ates his suffering by envisioning his lover as dead, while employing
heroic classical sun imagery as an architectonic element:

> This aristocrat, superb of all instinct,
>   With death close linked
> Has paced the enormous cloud, almost had won
>   War on the sun;
> Till now like Icarus mid-ocean-drowned
>   Hands, wings, are found.
>
> (*TP,* 3)

Still the overwhelming need is to possess his beloved. In "Saying
'good morning' becomes painful," conversation is "a form of possession
like taking your wrists" (*TP,* 13). To know what Marston is doing, to
dwell on his activities is yet another way to possess. In "Marston,
dropping it in the grate, broke his pipe" (*TP,* 8), the persona, in an
obvious Freudian gesture, builds possession on his knowledge of a pipe
that his friend had bought during a continental holiday and that had
given him much pleasure.

The young poet anoints himself God in "The Dust made Flesh" as he
describes creating four figures: Marston, Helen, Catherine, and Ainger,
a poet. Marston, close friend to the persona, thereby becomes a fabrica-
tion, perhaps because Spender wishes to back away from overt biographical exposure:

> First made I Marston the superb boxer
> More than with most men who dealt with death
> Marston who ski-ed through snow,
> Curved through the whiteness, ran,
> Helmeted drove through air.
>
> (*TP,* 4)

Marston's athleticism and purity are well established as the persona moves on to create "dark-eyed," cerebral Helen, with "words piercing night like stars," and the athletic Catherine, "who sprang in sky" and, like the goddess Diana, "along the ice-fleeced rocks shot chamois down." Spender certainly did not "make" Ainger, the poet, who is Auden cast as Byron—"severe, voiced raucous-reed, / With fascinating facets of crude mind, / An enormous percipient mass on the plain" (*TP,* 5). Spender was insecure and often ill at ease at Oxford, and thus liked to summarize his qualified admiration of friends with strong personalities, as if, by inference, he were deploring his own perceived lack of single-mindedness and ambition.

In "Acts passed beyond the boundary of mere wishing," the persona has tried to ingratiate himself with his lover, but the simple, ingenuous courtesy of "waiting for the tram" carrying his lover provokes gratitude and an explosion of ecstasy in the persona: "Thinking, if these were tricklings through a dam, / I must have love enough to run a factory on, / Or give a city power, or drive a train" (*TP,* 9).

In "I can never be a great man," one of the finest of the *Twenty Poems,* Spender comes out strongly against egotism as the proper motivating force behind great people. He proposes that those who rise above the rest of humanity do so through a complete selflessness that is far removed from the day-to-day working of body and mind. It is in the interior:

> Central "I" is surrounded by "I eating,"
> "I loving," "I angry," "I excreting,"
> And the "great I" planted in him
> Has nothing to do with all these.
>
> It can never claim its true place
> Resting in the forehead, and secure in his gaze.
> The "great I" is an unfortunate intruder
> Quarrelling with "I tiring" and "I sleeping"
> And all those other "I's" who long for "We dying."
>
> (*TP,* 17)

Although not immortal, the "great I," like a personified superego, has an energy and a love for life that serves in lieu of immortality. It tolerates all the weak, indolent, death-directed attitudes of body and mind, while making uncomfortable all the little "I's," the people who recognize that their drifting lives are wasted. Ultimately, "the first person singular can no longer be central; now the one who would seek fame must sink his personal identity in the first person plural."[10]

The "Marston Poems" after "The Dust made Flesh" either celebrate a man or address a man or a woman to whom the persona has an emotional attachment, but presumably it is Marston himself. Spender's early homoerotic poems, personal though they may be, are also a part of a tradition of such verse, a poetry that flowered in the trenches of World War I and was nearly as formalized and ritualized as the Renaissance sonnet sequence. Indeed, the great antecedent to these poems is Shakespeare's *Sonnets*.[11]

"Constant April" finds the persona lingering over the sensuous charms of his lover, relating him to the pleasant month:

> When you laughed, your laughter
> Was like the bright cascade.
> The sun sheds on a cloud,
>
> . . . .
>
> And if you frowned, your frowning
> Was knit as these
> Slight showers.
>
> (*TP*, 12)

Of course, platonic friendship and aesthetic appreciation are also expressed in "Constant April," as they are in "His Figure Passes" (*TP*, 6). The search for deep, sincere friendship is always a corollary to Spender's youthful passion for physical love and his need to find self-identity and worth in the reflections from a relationship.

The finest and most typically Spenderian poem in *Twenty Poems* is "The Port." Presumably a part of the "Marston Poems," it is really independent, describing the industrialized hub of commerce where sea, seashore, factory, and people meet. The port is where "the sea exerts his huge mandate" and where men work in "furnace" and "shipyards." As a collective image, the port is an objective correlative for the poet's frustration and unhappiness, manifest in the imagery of graves, caves, hard faces, lightning, confusion, and turmoil. The persona is of the industrial north. In the south, merchants dwell happily in "fat gardens" with "bronze-faced sons." In the port "the pale lily boys flaunt their bright lips, / Such pretty cups for money, and older whores / Scuttle rat-toothed into the dark outdoors" (*TP,* 14). For homosexuals and men who are disgusted with women and wavering on the sexual verge, the port is a titillating place full of sailors and boys.

"Written whilst walking down the Rhine"—which appears in subsequent collections as "In 1929"—shows Spender at his ceremonial best. The poem depicts the persona's friendship with two Germans, a bourgeois and a communist clerk. They are able to transcend the hatred their fathers felt in World War I:

> Our fathers killed. And yet there lives no feud
> Like Hamlet prompted on the castle stair;
> There falls no shade across our blank of peace
> We being together, struck across our path,
> Nor taper finger threatening solitude.
>
> (*TP,* 15)

However, if the past does not hinder, it nevertheless does not help, and separation is always the outcome:

> Lives risen a moment, joined or separate,
> Fall heavily, then are always separate,
> Stratum unreckoned by geologists,
> Sod lifted, turned, slapped back again with spade.
>
> (*TP,* 16)

This noble, haunting poem, notes D. E. S. Maxwell, "stands with the best work of Spender's contemporaries."[12]

In "Beethoven's Death Mask," also long recognized as superior Spender, the author again distances himself from a great person. He paints the composer as Rodin would have sculpted him, establishing depth, genius, mystery, and profundity:

> I imagine him still with heavy brow.
> Huge, black, with bent head and falling hair
> He ploughs the landscape. His face
> Is this hanging mask transfigured,
> This mask of the death which white lights make stare.

> I see the thick hands clasped; the scare-crow coat;
> The light strike upward at the holes for eyes.
>
> (*TP*, 23)

The persona remains fascinated by genius and the creative process that transforms experience and sound with negative capability. Spender explores the possibilities of spiritual aspiration through the achievement of Beethoven. He tries to imitate a master of music with the music and meaning of poetry:

> Then the drums move away, the Distance shows;
> Now cloud-hid peaks are bared; the mystic One
> Horizons haze, as the blue incense heaven.
> Peace, peace. . . . Then splitting skull and dream, there
>   comes
> Blotting our lights, the trumpeter, the sun.
>
> (*TP*, 23)

The horror, ugliness, and death behind the mask, with light (Spender's image source for creative energy) striking at "the hole for eyes," is mitigated by the poem's lyrical values, and thus the poem transforms itself and becomes its own subject.

Twenty Poems, although a youthful work, has humor, passionate intensity, deep feeling, clarity, and rich, concrete imagery. It is a quantum leap from *Nine Experiments* and would have been no small achievement for any poet, let alone a youth of 21.

Michael Roberts's *New Signatures*

In 1932 a young enthusiast of modern poetry, Michael Roberts, working with Leonard and Virginia Woolf at their Hogarth Press, put together an anthology of poems by young, recently discovered writers. The key poets were Spender, Auden, Day Lewis, William Empson, John Lehmann, and the American Richard Eberhart. Roberts's intention was to survey the imagery of modern life and to develop a new intellectual and imaginative synthesis that would deal positively with the problems of life in the twentieth century. The anthology was a great success, selling out quickly, and had to be reprinted in a few weeks. The book was hailed as a "manifesto of new poetry, and the poets within its pages found themselves lumped together in the imagination of readers as 'New Signatures poets.' "[13] *New Signatures* spawned *New Country* in 1933 and John Lehmann's magazine *New Writing,* which unlike the *Left Review* was more interested in literature than in politics.

Spender contributed more poetry to *New Signatures* than any of the other eight poets represented therein. Most of his seven contributions are part of the permanent canon of twentieth-century British poetry. Spender included all of them in *Poems* of 1933.

"The Express" is considered one of Spender's signature poems, embodying as it does the very essence of the aesthetics of the Pylon Poets: the transmutation of the antipoetic material of modern life into poetry. "The Express" is an art moderne painting in words. As in some Edward Hopper paintings, there are no people in this poem, wherein a train, a machine as terrible as death, is personified as a lovely woman:

> And always light, aeriel underneath
> Goes the elate metre of her wheels.
> Steaming through metal landscape on her lines
> She plunges new eras of wild happiness
> Where speed throws up strange shapes, broad curves
> And parallels clean like the steel of guns.
>
> (*NS,* 92)

For the train and the plane and the gasworks are more significant in modern life than the fields and forms of ancient song: "Ah, like a comet through flame, she moves entranced / Wrapped in her music no bird song, no, nor bough / Breaking with honey bud, shall ever equal" (*NS,* 93). The train "acquires mystery" and "she begins to sing." Then she screams and is heard "further than Edinburgh or Rome / Beyond the crest of the world." Here is orgasm. Here, too, is political élan, for the express symbolizes the force of "the first, powerful, plain manifesto" driving the revolution to its appointment with destiny.

"The Funeral" is one of Spender's great short poems in which lyric sensibility wars manifestly with political statement. It is vintage Spender, as is "The Landscape near an Aerodrome" written a short while later. Spender is fascinated with the processes and products of industry, and he both admires and envies the workers in factory and mill. The virile pride in the description of the funeral of the worker who "excelled all others in making drivingbelts" and the future that his labor has

made possible sound like an anthem and recalls huge Soviet posters of
the 1930s and 1940s:

> They walk home remembering the straining red flags;
> And with pennons of song fluttering through their blood
> They dream of the World State
> With its towns like brain-centres and its pulsing
> arteries.
>
> (NS, 95)

Later on Spender would find the overtness of poems like "The Funeral"
somewhat embarrassing and would include them in anthologies and
collections only because the public expected to see them there, but the
fact is that youthful panache and the lyric fusion of romantic and
modern images continue to thrill new readers, especially the young and
idealistic.

"I Think Continually" is an elegiac poem reminiscent of Laurence
Binyon's "For the Fallen." With exquisite phrasing, Spender admires
those strong personalities who are so unified that a single expression
may be their apt signature. The great are imagistically with fire and
sun in their struggle to aid and to save their fellow humans:

> The names of those who in their lives fought for life,
> —Who wore at their hearts the flame's centre:
> Born of the sun, they travelled a short while towards
> the sun
> And left the vivid air signed with their honour.
>
> (NS, 90)

These are the people with a destiny, who bring with them from the
spiritual realm of perfection a memory of glory:

> I think continually of those who were truly great.
> Who, from the womb, remembered the soul's history
> Through corridors of light where the hours are suns
> Endless and singing. Whose lovely ambition
> Was that their lips, still touched with fire,
> Should tell of the Spirit clothed from head to foot in
> song.
>
> (NS, 89)

Spender may not be one of the truly great, and the poem may express
a degree of envy and resignation, but the awareness of the spiritual

dimension of greatness is of significance. "Who lives under the shadow of war" reminds the reader that Spender's generation is an interwar group of survivors. The young poet knows that no writer's words can stop the next war.

"On Young Men" is a poem of political commitment exhorting his fellow youth to leave "those ladies like flies perfect in amber" and "those financiers like fossils of bones in coal" to "advance to rebuild" their society, not forgetting to "sleep with friend on hill" (NS, 86). The images are intense and precise, but also somewhat labored, and one recalls MacNeice's mean description of Spender as a poet patiently pressing clichés into poetic shape with steady and powerful hands. [14] Spender did "press" in much of his earliest poetry, but he pressed metaphysical imagery, not clichés.

"My Parents" deplores an upbringing that separated him from boys of the working class and made him their perceived enemy: "My parents kept me from children who were rough." The persona came to fear them when they "sprang out behind hedges / Like dogs to bark at our world." He "longed to forgive them, but they never smiled" (NS, 94).

"The Prisoners" is a weaker poem, flabbily self-referential and unable to evoke much of a credible sense of life in prison. The employment of the pathetic fallacy does not help. It is hard to imagine a "liquid door / Melted with anger" (NS, 87). Perhaps the persona or the prisoners are melting it with their anger.

It is easy to see how Spender's committed, exuberant poems excited a poetry-reading public in the early 1930s seeking a poetry of social hope, a public prepared to sort out and grace the machine-dominated environment it seemed somehow to have wandered into.

Michael Robert's next anthology, New Country (1933), contains four personal Spender poems, but they are not as distinguished as his contributions to New Signatures. One, "The morning road with the electric trains," Spender dropped from the canon immediately. "At the end of two month's holiday there came a night," "Alas, when he laughs it is not he," and "After success, your little afternoon, success" were included in the second edition of the 1933 Poems, as were all of the New Signatures pieces.

Poems

Poems (1933) contains 33 poems of which 16 had appeared in previous volumes, including New Signatures and New Country. Changes are minor. The second edition of *Poems*, published in September 1934, contains 40 poems, Spender having dropped 2 ("I hear the cries of evening" and "My parents quarrel in the neighbour room") and added 9 ("At the end of two months' holiday," "After success, your little afternoon success," "Alas, when he laughs it is not he," "The Shapes of Death," "For T.A.H.R.," "Van der Lubbe," "Passing, men are sorry for the birds in cages," "Perhaps," and "New Year"). The 1934 American edition, Spender's first book published in the United States, restored the 2 omitted poems. The American edition is considered definitive.

Within two years of the publication of *Poems*, Morton Zabel, in *Poetry*, called Spender "one of the most important young poets in England," one who would prove to be "a writer not only of immediate values but of permanent and convincing truth."[15] *Poems* is an estimable achievement, projecting an exuberant quality to be long remembered and happily recalled, like Shelley's, that of a young bard of wide-eyed affirmation. "The naïveté *is* Spender . . . it goes along with a genuine innocence of eye, and a capacity not only for being easily moved, but for honouring that emotion in strong and direct expression."[16]

Variations of subject and style abound in *Poems;* rhetorical declamations, conversations, commentaries on current issues and public events, and psychological portraits intermingle. "The Express," "The Pylons" and "The Landscape near an Aerodrome" employ imagery from modern technology instead of from traditional, outdated sources. The eponymous pylons, carrying electrical power above a valley, introduce the landscape of the future: "Like whips of anger / With lightning's danger / There runs the quick perspective of the future."[17] Nature is diminished by the power of human ingenuity, and the anthropomorphized pylons take on an aura of sexuality:

> Now over these small hills they have built the concrete
> That trails black wire:
> Pylons, those pillars
> Bare like nude, giant girls that have no secret.
>
>   (*P,* 57)

"The Landscape near an Aerodrome" depicts the changing concept of what is beautiful and fascinating, turning away from traditional landscape, ruined towns, and the displays of religion, to the sleek, streamlined machines of speed and mechanical power. A descending airliner is like a great eagle alighting:

> More beautiful and soft than any moth
> With burring furred antennae feeling its huge path
> Through dusk, the air-liner with shut-off engines
> Glides over suburbs and the sleeves set trailing tall
> To point the wind. Gently, broadly, she falls
> Scarcely disturbing charted currents of air.
>
> (P, 55)

The passengers now can see the ruins that rampant, uncaring, capitalistic industrialization has wrought:

> now let their eyes trained by watching
> Penetrate through dusk the outskirts of this town
> Here where industry shows a fraying edge.
> Here they may see what is being done.
>
> (P, 55)

Finally, as the earth images grow larger and larger,

> Beyond the winking masthead light
> And the landing-ground, they observe the outposts
> Of work: chimneys like lank black fingers
> Or figures frightening and mad: and squat buildings
> With their strange air behind trees, like women's faces
> Shattered by grief.
>
> (P, 55)

And they find a "landscape of hysteria" where a church is blocking that imagistic source of creativity and love, the sun:

> Then, as they land, they hear the tolling bell
> Reaching across the landscape of hysteria
> To where, larger than all the charcoaled batteries
> And imaged towers against that dying sky,
> Religion stands, the church blocking the sun.
>
> (P, 56)

The message is to have faith in the new forces symbolized by train, plane, and pylon and to abandon the old institutions like the church because they block the guiding light to the future.

In "In railway halls" and "Moving through the silent crowd" Spender paints a drama of despair in which institutions created for the welfare of humans have failed and the pitiful poor have nothing but time: "In railway halls, on pavements near the traffic, / They beg, their eyes made big by empty staring / And only measuring Time, like the blank clock" (P, 60).

The unemployed teem on the streets in "Moving through the silent crowd":

> They lounge at corners of the street
> And greet friends with a shrug of shoulder
> And turn their empty pockets out,
> The cynical gestures of the poor.
>
> (P, 30)

The predominant emotion in these early poems is pity. This recurring theme, the keystone of Spender's poetry, is partly a result of the influence of Wilfred Owen, who took as his subject pity for the suffering soldiers in war. Spender pitied the suffering of the victims of economic crisis.[18]

Another iterative Spender theme consolidated in *Poems* is the primary significance of personal relations in life. In poems like "Those fireballs, those ashes" and the earlier "Oh young men" and "I think continually," Spender emphasizes the centrality of the physical aspect of human greatness. The sensuous being comes first. Relationships must have their physical dimensions, and this is true for great and small. Friends and lovers are more vital to physical and mental health, artistic achievement, and political action than are family, country, ideals, or ideology. MacNeice recalls Spender's "building what castles he could out of personal relations."[19] The power of the intimate exalted all.

"For T.A.R.H.," somewhat revised later, is based on Spender's relationship with his sometime secretary, Tony Hyndman, but primarily deals with the poet's inner-world reaction to the creative and destructive powers of love and to love's capacity to induce forgiveness:

> At night my life lies with no past nor future
> But only space. It watches
> Hope and despair and the small vivid longings
> Like minnows gnaw the body. Where it drank love
> It lives in sameness. Here are
> Gestures indelible.
>
> (P, 36)

"How strangely this sun reminds me of my love" finds the persona staring longingly at the other male's face, taking his photograph, so to speak, with the retinas of his eyes in order to remember the glorious day. The young lover is like the god Apollo.

In "Your body is stars whose million glitter here," a lover is anatomized metaphorically as Spender uses parataxis to paint a surrealistic canvas:

> Your body is stars whose million glitter here:
> I am lost amongst the branches of this sky
> Here near my breast, here in my nostrils, here
> Where our vast arms like streams of fire lie.
>
> (*P*, 35)

Unfortunately, the plethora of images seems to melt and drip, and when in the end "there comes the shutting of a door," the reader does not know on what it shuts.

"What I expected" debunks the youthful fancy of the poet's heroic self-image:

> What I expected was
> Thunder, fighting,
> Long struggles with men
> And climbing.
> After continual straining
> I should grow strong;
> Then the rocks would shake
> And I should rest long.
>
> (*P*, 25)

Alas, he could not foresee the common fate of love and life: "The pulverous grief / Melting the bones with pity, / The sick falling from earth" (*P*, 25–26).

"Without that once clear aim, the path of flight" despairs that the twentieth century is like the Dark Ages, in that social and psychological truth lie both "in dungeons" of the mind and the real dungeons of political repression. Another type of repression is dealt with in "Passing, men are sorry for the birds in cages." Here the persona is able to announce the release of "the bird of delight" from its cage and denounce the false ideas that have kept it in prison. Those who lock up the joys of life destroy themselves.

"Van der Lubbe," named for the innocent defendant tried by the Nazis on a trumped-up charge of causing the Reichstag fire, is a political poem emphasizing the correlation between public and private Thanatos, which together shape the destructive element in humankind. Other very political poems are "Perhaps," in which several violent acts take place, their settings, time, and purpose remaining vague. "After they have tired" expects the revolution to bring a dazzling dawn without banks, cathedrals, and insane rulers. In "New Year" the persona urges the oppressed to rise up and create that new dawn but "effect . . . beauty without robbery" (*P,* 64). Spender is always a little chary of revolution; he cannot accommodate himself to the bloodshed.

"My parents quarrel in the neighbour room," which complements "My parents kept me from children who were rough," from *New Signatures,* is a miniature version of George Meredith's *Modern Love.* The persona, here a horrified son, listens to his parents wage war in their bedroom.

The last poem in the collection, "Not palaces, an era's crown," is an awkward Marxist piece with some foolish metaphors, such as a "battleship towering from hilly waves." Yet the poem is also a call to duty. The poet instructs his senses and his readers' to abandon their "gardens" and their "singing feasts" and submit to the design of the will to serve the "flag of our purpose" (*P,* 67).

Despite the seemingly political nature of much of *Poems,* a large percentage of the pieces are about self. In one sense, the collection is a course in personal analysis, the self being reconciled with internal needs and social concerns. The id and the superego struggle but accommodate. After all, if Marx saw change as predicated on material forces in society, Freud believed that change was motivated by forces within the individual. In *Civilization and Its Discontents* (1930) Freud is concerned with a person's relation to his guilt and to his society. In respect to the latter, Spender's early poems are as much Freudian as they are Marxist. The widespread fascination with Freud in the 1930s could no more have escaped Spender's attention than it did Auden's.

Poems is a remarkable achievement for a very young poet in a great hurry to get things said. Samuel Hynes, in *The Auden Generation,* poses a key question that imaginative writers faced throughout the 1930s: "Is the role of a poet a defensible one in such a time? And if it is, what sort of poem should he write? Is the traditional private context of lyric poetry appropriate . . . to a time of public distress?"[20] Spender's answer in *Poems* is a resounding yes. A lyric could be both private and public, both a song and a manifesto. This was the accomplishment of *Poems:* capturing the interest of a British public still exhausted by World War I, still grieving over the decimation of the brightest of a generation, and continually disappointed with its leadership. That public wanted to understand the inherent nature, the psychological makeup, and the source of energy of the inspiring figures of the human race, "those who were truly great." *Poems* addressed the need.

Vienna

Vienna (1934) is Spender's grand attempt to project into public view "the conflict between personal life and public causes" (*WW,* 174). The experiences of a love relationship and the poet's indignation at the suppression of the Viennese Socialists by Prime Minister Engelbert Dollfuss were different but related, for although one was public and one private, both were intensely emotional and personal. Spender felt "the poem fails because it does not fuse the two halves of a split situation, and attain a unity where the inner passion becomes inseparable from the outer one" (*WW,* 174).

In *Poems* the cure for human ills lies in making the individual more happy and more aware of instincts, freeing sexuality, and developing emotional potential. In *Vienna* Spender explicitly considers the notion of "individual love as a cultural panacea" and then rejects it "in favor of a Marxist program."[21]

The four-part, 37-page *Vienna* is Spender's longest and most ambitious poem. It, more than any other work of his, shows Eliot's influence. The fact that Spender not only spent so much time in Austria and Germany but also chose to set his "epic" in a Central European capital at what he immediately recognized as a pivotal place and point in twentieth-century European history underscores Eliot's position that English "writers cannot afford to throw over the European tradition."[22] In Eliot's view, the English artist needs to turn his or her mind east to the Continent and away from the west (America) and the world (the British Empire). For Spender's generation of poets *The Waste Land* was the great "epic" of the century. In Spender's construct and interpretation of events, Vienna, embattled, gutted, and raped of its hope, becomes a "wasteland" in which the dream of a socialist civilization perishes. Vienna is, then, symbolic of the European cities in which the lights of political and individual freedom were going out in the 1930s. *Vienna* is a prophecy. The very imagery of the poem is Eliotic, with strings of images sequencing in emotional rather than logical iterations while fulfilling the precept of the objective correlative.

The first section of the poem, "Arrival at the City," describes the persona's coming to Vienna, where he takes up residence in the Pension Beaurepas, in which most of the inhabitants are old ladies who prattle on about their medical problems and elderly lovers. The proprietor, an ex-actor who likes to pass as an Englishman and who wishes to introduce the persona to his obscene version of *panen et circenses* (bread and circuses)—*"penis in circensem."*[23] The proprietor, a faded dandy, sports "wing tie. Winged nose. A bleared, active eye. / The stick and strut of a sprucer day" (V, 10). But "this man's dead life stinking" is like an open wound decaying. He is so obscene that the persona prefers "the wholly dead" to the living corpse and bag of corruption.

The persona wanders to another part of the city, a square quarter that is "the part true to this town" (V, 12). It is like a hospital for a sick city:

> Unhomely windows, floors scrubbed clean of love,
> A waste canvas sky, uniformed nuns,
> Streets tinkling with the silver ambulance.
> We breathe the bandaged air and watch through
>   windows
> Metal limbs, glass eyes, ourselves frozen on
>   fires.
>
>   (V, 12)

"Arrival at the City" thus provides the backdrop for the tragedy of the oppression and murder of a decayed city, whose sacrifice may provide understanding and inspiration for those trying to prevent the death of Western civilization.

The second section, "Parade of the Executive," is even more abstract than the first. The suggestion of a foreign journalist surveying and recording the degeneration of an exotic city, like Isherwood in Berlin, disappears as the poem metamorphoses into a position paper by "the Executive," who advocates obedience to the dictator and his henchmen and the maintenance of appearances:

> Let no one disagree let Dollfuss
> Fey, Stahremberg, the whole bloody lot
> Appear frequently, shaking hands at street corners
> Looking like bad sculptures of their photographs.
> Let there be bands and stands and preparations

> And grateful peasants in costumed deputations
> Create the ghost of an emperor's coronation
> Stalking the streets and holding up the trams.
>
> (V, 14)

Meanwhile, there are the unemployed who are

> Dispersed like idle points of a vague star:
> Huddled on benches, nude at bathing places,
> And made invisible by crucifying suns
> Day after day, again with grief afire at night,
> They do not watch what we show.
> Their eyes are fixed upon an economic margin.
>
> (V, 14)

And there is a stranger, an observer, "a witness free from danger," like Spender, who sees a government minister, after a deceitful public event "who smiles and smiles." The stranger cries out like Hamlet, "How now! a rat? Dead for a ducat" (V, 20). The city of Vienna is as rotten as the state of Denmark.

The third part, "The Death of Heroes," describes the brave attempt and tragic failure of the workers and students who fought the fascists at Karl-Marx-Hof. This section of the poem is most powerful and stirring as it describes the suffering of the besieged. The slaughter is appalling: "Life seems black against the snow." A sniper fires and "the vivid runner falls / From his hare-breathed anxiety: his undisputing / Hold on terror. O gently, whitely buried" (V, 25). In the end the beaten and burrowing survivors without "tasks fit for heroes" must find new roles and "change death's signal honour for a life of moles" (V, 30). The dead are lucky; they are not dehumanized by the loss of freedom.

In the fourth part, "Analysis and Final Statement," the persona, the stranger, like a Prufrock, listens to coffeehouse voices, trying to understand, excuse, exculpate, and somehow assimilate what has happened around him. The persona, however, loses his frayed journalistic objectivity, his voyeuristic perspective, and turns inward to "I, I, I" and the love of a woman in order to heal his psyche:

> I think often of a woman
> With dark eyes neglected, a demanding turn of the
>   head
> And hair of black silky beasts.

> How admirable it is
> They offer a surface bright as fruit in rain
> That feeds on kissing. Loving is their conqueror
> That turns all sunshine, fructifying lemons.
>
> (V, 33)

The heterosexuality that has been repressed in the persona, but leaks out in the description by the elderly ladies in the pension of their gray loves, in the proprietor's lust, and in other sexual references, blossoms into the conscious understanding that "our sexes are the valid flowers / Sprinkled across the total world and wet / With night" (V, 34).

Unlike Eliot's *The Waste Land,* published 12 years earlier, Spender's *Vienna* does not present a coherent, overall vision. Its obscurity seems imposed. However, as Samuel Hynes points out, "*Vienna* is a poem not so much about the history of the uprising as about the mythology. It is not a narrative, though it includes narrative passages: it does not tell the whole story, it ignores chronology, and it does not explain. What Spender seems to have aimed at was the expression of his own personal sense of Vienna."[24]

The Still Centre

The Still Centre (1939) contains 39 poems written between 1934 and 1939. They are grouped into four parts and preceded by a forward in which Spender explains that the poems in Part One were the first written and are subject-oriented. Parts Two and Three contain political poems, the last of which are concerned with Spain. Part Four is not directly referred to, but Spender states that the violence of the times he was living in and the need for action could make a writer feel that writing was "perhaps something that he is ashamed of. For this reason, in my most recent poems [the bulk of Part Four], I have deliberately turned back to a kind of writing which is more personal, and I have included within my subjects weakness and fantasy and illusion."[25] No more *Viennas* for him. Intrepid Spender flew in the face of expectations: he would write a song of himself when all thought he would continue to engage in political battle with fascism. Disillusionment with communism may have partly caused this turn, but the change was primarily the result of an unleashing of the pent-up romantic in the poet. Spender had come to feel that he was his own manifesto. As Eliot fled from the wasteland to religion and as Auden ran away to America to escape the coming chaos, Spender retreated to the still center on the isle of self.

Speaking of *The Still Centre,* David Daiches says, "The vein of lyrical speculation in this volume sometimes produces poetry which can hold its own with anything produced in the century."[26] The collection's value was immediately recognized, receiving such critical accolades as "the best work of one of the most competent and sincere of living poets."[27]

The title of the collection derives from Spender's sense of living on "the edge of being," on the periphery of events in the 1930s. "I had always the sense of living on the circumference of a circle at whose centre I could never be" (*WW,* 174–75). In *The Still Centre,* Spender is here less concerned with relating the self to the outside world. Instead, like Rainer Maria Rilke, he strives to convert external phenomena into symbols of the inner experience: "Ideally, the artist should transform the environment into his own world."[28] Looking out the window of a train he sees his image against the traveling landscape. That outside world is fleeting and unreal.

In the introduction to *The Still Centre,* Spender says that "poetry does not state truth, it states the conditions within which something felt is true. Even while he is writing about the little portion of reality which is part of his experience, the poet may be conscious of a different reality outside. His problem is to relate the small truth to the sense of a wider, perhaps theoretically known truth outside his experience" (*SC,* 10). Spender had struggled throughout the decade from pre-Oxford isolation through fervent desire for social action, to political disappointment, and finally to a renewal of hope for human survival, humanistic values, and personal love.

Part One's rather didactic poetry begins with "Polar Exploration," an early-1930s poem in which arctic explorers march through a world of white to winter quarters, exploring the realm of male relationships as much as external nature. Their intense lives contrast with the dull, bourgeois existence at home. The persona has come to realize that he is symbolically living in a new Ice Age: "Was / Ice our anger transformed?" But the more evil place "Is the North / Over there," presumably Germany, with "a tangible, real madness" and led by "A glittering simpleton" (*SC,* 18), an underestimation of Hitler.

"Easter Monday," another early poem in the collection, is a political piece. On the day after the Resurrection

> The bourgeois in tweeds
> Holds in his golden spectacles'
> Twin lenses, the velvet and far

> Mountains. But look, rough hands
> From trams, 'buses, bicycles, and of tramps,
> Like one hand red with labour, grasp
> The furred and future bloom
> Of their falling, falling world.
>
> (*SC*, 19–20)

The Resurrection is like a revolution, but the "one hand red with labour," not with blood, will shape the future. The political position is more Fabian than Marxian.

The important love motive in *The Still Centre* begins with "Experience." Indeed, love is the ultimate "centre" the poet seeks. In obtaining experience, the persona bids farewell to childhood, to the "headaching" world before heterosexual experience, and enters the new world of Eros in which exists "two people . . . and both double, yet different. I entered with myself, I left with a woman" (*SC*, 21).

For C. Day Lewis the following lines were "pure poetry," impossible to transcribe into prose without impairing meaning:[29]

> Good-bye now, good-bye: to the early and sad hills
> Dazed with their houses, like a faint migraine.
> Orchards bear memory in cloudy branches.
> The entire world roars in a child's brain.
>
> (*SC*, 21–22)

One of Spender's "obsessive themes" is the unity of being. Humans struggle toward that state. Some may achieve the condition of unity after death. "Exiles from Their Land, History Their Domicile" is "about those who have, after their deaths, obtained for their lives a symbolic significance which certainly passed unnoticed when they were living."[30] Death chooses purposes and actions that give lives symbolic significance: "What miracle divides / Our purpose from our weakness?" (*SC*, 25). Great historical exiles bring their values to bear on the present. They are "freedom's friends." Although they "were jokes to children," their will, their courage, "their deeds and deaths are birds" (*SC*, 24). The persona prays to them:

> Recall me from life's exile, let me join
> Those who now kneel to kiss their sands,
> And let my words restore
> Their printed, laurelled, victoried message.
>
> (*SC*, 25)

Spender yet thinks "continually of those who were truly great."

In "The Past Values," retitled "The Living Values" in *Collected Poems, 1928–1953,* the past is challenged as being destructive. The glazed look in the portraits of old masters appears like "the eyes of the freshly young dead / sprawled in the mud of battle" (*SC, 26*). A metaphysical conceit locks together the sad eyes of the inspirers, the dusty glass over portraits, the fog, and those poor soldiers "struck . . . with lead so swift / Their falling sight stared through its glass" (*SC, 27*). At the same time, "The Past Values" laments that modern war perverts and destroys the greatness of our legacy. Eros and Thanatos ever entwine. The old masters inspire creation and destruction, for they have also left us the patriotism and lust that have brought young soldiers to their deaths and ended their "dream of girls."

Although close to propaganda, "An Elementary School Class Room in a Slum" presents the poet's sincere concern for the social anomoly of children with their future "painted with a fog." Shakespeare and geography are meaningless to hungry children who "wear skins peeped through by bones and spectacles of steel / with mended glass." Their maps are blotted "with slums as big as doom" (*SC, 29*). The poem succeeds because of its sheer lyrical quality, its deep pity, its justifiable anger, and its prescription for the salvation of all parties to the social contract: create a Laurentian world for children where sensation and intellect unite to "break the town" and find a history "whose language is the sun," while the children joyously "let their tongues / Run naked into books" (*SC, 29*).

Because it is also about children and rebirth, "A Footnote (from Marx's Chapter on the Working Day)" in Part Two is discussed here. At the opening, children in school mouth foolishness and errors until, as in the speeches of Lear's Fool, the images have deeper meaning than the denotation:

> "So perhaps all the people are dead, and we're birds
> "Shut in steel cages by the devil who's good,
> "Like the miners in their pit cages
> "And us in our chimneys to climb, as we should."
>
> (*SC, 43*)

Children in their "angel infancy" are indeed birds, and the adults are dead, their souls imprisoned in error. Yet the children, with instinctive cognition, understand their tragic fate.

The last poem in Part One, "The Uncreated Chaos," in four parts and
84 lines, is the second longest and one of the most significant in the
collection. In it Spender expresses what for him was the great modern
dilemma: being drawn toward the will and the world in which it is
operative while simultaneously desiring to escape both will and world
to the still center.

The world requires our obeisance: "To the hanging despair of eyes in
the street, offer / Your making hands and your guts on skewers of pity"
(*SC*, 30). At the same time, we poor spirits feed a fantasy:

> When the pyramid sky is piled with clouds of sand
>   which the yellow
> Sun blasts above, respond to that day's doom
> With a headache. Let your ghost follow
> The young men to the Pole, up Everest, to war: by
>   love, be shot.
>
> (*SC*, 30)

But always "the uncreating chaos" of modern life descends upon us and
destroys integrity while promoting selfishness, vanity, and hedonism:

> For the uncreating chaos descends
> And claims you in marriage: though a man, you were
>   ever a bride:
> Ever beneath the supple surface of summer muscle,
> The fountain evening talk cupping the summer stars,
> The student who chucks back the lock from his hair
>   in front of a silver glass,
> You were only anxious that all these passions should
>   last.
>
> (*SC*, 30)

Part of the uncreating chaos, developing like a cosmic storm, is the
rise of the Nazis, a truly destructive element:

> Meagre men shoot up. Rockets, rockets,
> A corporal's [Hitler] fiery tongue wags about burning
>   parliament.
> There flows in the tide of killers, the whip-masters,
> Breeches and gaiters camouflage blood.
>
> (*SC*, 32–33)

What is to be done when a terrible world is too much with us? One does one's work. That is the only answer. One changes what one can and returns to "the simple mechanism. . . . Clear day, thoughts of the work-room, the desk, / The hand, symbols of power" (*SC,* 33). The progress of "The Uncreating Chaos" is in the desperate struggle between the archetypal forces of creation and destruction, with human love on the I-Thou scale the saving grace and the hope of rebirth. Thus, "The Uncreating Chaos" is the turning point in Spender's poetry. The poet has defined his work: it is poetry. The cost in isolation must be borne.

Part Two of *The Still Centre* is a miscellany of Marxist poems, sketches, love poems, and typical Spender machinery pieces, such as "View from a Train" and "The Midlands Express." These, along with "Houses at Edge of Railway Lines" in Part Four, show that Spender had not quite finished with what Auden called the "strict beauty of locomotive."

"View from a Train" again finds the persona seeing himself reflected in a train's window superimposed upon the landscape and remembering that the "man behind his mask still wears a child." "The Midlands Express" is another "The Express." This train is a "Muscular Virtuoso!" and very sexy, for "all England lies beneath you like a woman / With limbs ravished" (*SC,* 47). The train is compared, not quite convincingly, to "great art. . . . Whose giant travelling ease / Is the vessel of its effort and fatigue" (*SC,* 47).

In "Houses at Edge of Railway Lines" the persona looks for love while journeying on a train. It is "an age of bombs" and the passengers search for "hope on the horizon," but the persona, looking elsewhere, wishes "without knocking to enter / The life that lies behind / the edges of drawn blinds" (*SC,* 103), as if he were a lover calling. In the tranquil home we all long for "love fills rooms, as gold / Pours into a valid mould" (*SC,* 103).

"Hoelderlin's Old Age," like "Beethoven's Death Mask," is an elegy and a celebration of old age and evening. In the German romantic tradition, the old poet Johann Hölderlin defies death's power as his "soul sings / Burning vividly in the centre of a cold sky" (*SC,* 37). Hölderlin has found his still center.

Three poems in Part Two are quite personal. "Hampstead Autumn" is a childhood reminiscence of a mature man who sorts out what he can and what he cannot regain from the past. In the end, the sun sets on "images, / Continuous and fragile as China" (*SC,* 38). The four-line "In the Street" is unusually aphoristic for Spender. The persona comes out in favor of isolation, "a blank wall with my self face to face," having grown weary of "the lies and lights of the complex street" (*SC*, 39). "In the Street" counters the sentimentality of "Hampstead Autumn" with existential self-reliance. "The Room on the Square" finds a rejected lover accepting his isolation as he climbs to "the dark room / Which hangs above the square." Again, as in "Houses at the Edge of Railway Lines," the persona sees love happening elsewhere and to others, and he misses it sorely. The dark room once had a "light in the window [that] seemed perpetual" (*SC*, 40) because love was there for him. Yet love and loss are natural to the human experience, begetting growth.

"The Indifferent One" and "Three Days" are also love poems about loss. Although personal and obscure in their reference, they remain accessible in emotion, description, and sensuality. The former asks the loved one for "the smile's indifference which forgives" (*SC*, 49), and the latter finds the persona reminiscing on "sensual memories" and "your image and those days of glass" (*SC*, 51).

"The Marginal Field" is a socialist poem that deplores the exploitation of the farmer, but strained language militates against the message, although the opening stanza is lyrically fine, presenting yet again a view through a glass:

> On the chalk cliff edge struggles the final field
> Of barley smutted with tares and marbled
> With veins of rusted poppy as though the plough
>   had bled.
> The sun is drowned in bird-wailing mist,
> The sea and sky meet outside distinction,
> The landscape glares and stares—white poverty
> Of gaslight diffused through frosted glass.
>
> (*SC*, 41)

"Thoughts during an Air Raid" really belongs among Spender's poems of the Spanish Civil War in Part Three, the strongest, most significant, and most famous section of *The Still Centre*. These war poems show the strong influence of the soldier poet of pity, Wifred Owen. Unlike Owen, Spender was an observer of war, not a participant, and thus in his war poems he balances emotional reactions with his lifelong antiwar commitment. The sheer honesty of these war poems is compelling. "Some of them are among the most celebrated poems of the war."[31] "Thoughts during an Air Raid" finds the persona, "the great 'I,' " in a hotel bed in Madrid wondering if "a bomb should dive / Its nose right through this bed" (*SC,* 45). The persona, truly and reasonably frightened, tries to be flippant when confronted by the thought of imminent death. He generalizes his experiences into the terror most humans have at the thought of their own ending, but "horror is postponed / For everyone until it settles on him" (*SC,* 45). Solipsism is, after all, a defense against the anonymity of death. Even a Stalingrad is for one participant an individual experience. One wonders how many thousands of Londoners recalled this poem during the Blitz?

Part Three, mislocated in the Contents, really begins with "Two Armies," a recollection of the bitterness of war in winter wherein "two armies / Dig their machinery" and "men freeze and hunger" (*SC,* 55). Yet, in war there is also much serenity between battles. The imagery borders on the erotic in a scene reminiscent of Shakespeare's *Henry V:*

> Clean silence drops at night when a little walk
> Divides the sleeping armies, each
> Huddled in linen woven by remote hands.
> When the machines are stilled, a common suffering
> Whitens the air with breath and makes both one
> As though these enemies slept in each other's arms.
>
> (*SC,* 56)

Clarity bursts over Spender's war poetry like a flare in the night. "Two Armies" dominates the panorama of war. More intimate scenes, comparable to cinematic close-ups, come later.

The sardonic "Ultima Ratio Regum" (The final argument of kings) describes the death of an insignificant, unknown soldier killed in a cause he did not comprehend: "The boy lying dead under the olive trees / Was too young and too silly / To have been notable to their important eye." The next line, so shocking, emphasizes the odd eroticism of war: "He was a better target for a kiss" (*SC,* 57). Yet war is foolish and wasteful:

> Consider. One bullet in ten thousand kills a man.
> Ask. Was so much expenditure justified
> On the death of one so young and so silly
> Lying under the olive trees, O world, O death?
>
> (*SC,* 58)

There are no heroes or heroics in Spender's view of war. In that sense, he is an "antiwar poet" rather than a "war poet," and in World War II he would pointedly refuse the proffered role of war poet. In the introduction to *The Still Centre* Spender makes it clear that he cannot write about heroism because it was not his experience (*SC*, 10). He could write about pity. That he knew. So did Wilfred Owen, who said, "My subject is war and the pity of war. The poetry is in the pity."[32]

For a noncombatant—perhaps because he could keep some distance, physically and emotionally—Spender's war imagery is unusually evocative: "The unflowering wall sprouted with guns, / Machine-gun anger quickly scythed the grasses" (*SC*, 57). His only American equal in this kind of imagery is Randall Jarrell in such poems as "The Death of the Ball Turret Gunner."

"The Coward" shows the persona's pity for a soldier who has destroyed his whole life in a moment of cowardice: "I gather all my life and pour / Out its love and comfort here" (*SC*, 60). The referential image is of a soldier emptying his canteen. But there is a drop of human kindness left for him. The persona states, "My love and pity shall not cease / for a lifetime at least" (*SC*, 60). Spender was accused of being a tourist at war.[33] Unfair! He was committed to the Spanish Republic, and his anguish was as real as anyone's. By his own admission, he would not have been much of a soldier.

In the fine poem "A Stopwatch and an Ordinance Map," Spender again depicts the death of a soldier, one who will no longer need to know the time and place. A moment of violence and pain "and the bones are fixed at five / Under the moon's timelessness" (*SC*, 61).

"War Photograph" is surely a commentary on the most famous photo of the Spanish Civil War, Robert Capa's picture of a Republican soldier at the moment he was shot: "the instant lurks / With its metal fang planned for my heart" (*SC*, 62). The dying soldier knows that the ultimate photo is taken by fate: "My corpse be covered with the snows' December / And roots push through skin's silent drum / When the years and fields forget, but the whitened bones remember" (*CS*, 63). Perhaps to avoid the Capa connection, Spender changed the poem's title to "In No Man's Land" and shortened the piece in *Collected Poems, 1928–1953*.

In the Petrarchan "Sonnet" the persona criticizes the world for looking at his lover as a surface image "moving upon the social glass of silver" (*SC*, 64), but he plunges through those mirrored rays to his lover's "hidden inner self." The persona cannot solve the troubles of the world, but he can drown in the life of his love.

"Fall of a City" depicts the despair of a city that falls to the fascists. Although probably about Madrid, the poem prophesies the fall of Prague, Warsaw, and Paris in World War II. Perhaps the greatest loss is to culture:

> All the names of heroes in the hall
> Where the feet thundered and the bronze throats
>   roared,
> Fox and Lorca claimed as history on the walls,
> Are now angrily deleted
> Or to dust surrender their dust,
> From golden praise excluded.
>
> > (*SC*, 65)

While for the poor children "all the lessons learned, [are] unlearnt" (*SC*, 66). Finally, though, the next generation must find the "spark from the days of energy." It did. Spain is now free. It may be because the Spanish child of the late 1930s hoarded liberty's energy "like a bitter toy" (*SC*, 66).

"At Castellon" (referring to a large Mediterranean port 50 miles north of Valencia) evokes the desperately tense atmosphere of a city about to be bombed. A worker is asked to drive the poet to the next village. They leave behind them what "the winged black roaring gates unload. / Cargoes of iron and of fire" (*SC*, 68). "The Bombed Happiness" presents an extended metaphor of the result of a bomb burst on children, who are turned into dancing harlequins by the force of the blast. Their flesh is stripped and "their blood twisted in rivers of song" (*SC*, 69). The state has played cruelly with these children. Its "toy was human happiness" (*SC*, 70). "At Castellon" and "The Bombed Happiness" are both rhymed pieces, unusual for Spender, who recognized that rhyme was not his forte. The delicacy of rhyme seems inappropriate for these violent poems.

"Port Bou," which takes its title from the small Spanish port that was Spender's entry point from France (*WW*, 199) and that had been bombed before he arrived, skillfully sums up the themes and attitudes of the Spanish Civil War poems. The extended metaphor of the poem is a broken circle representing the open bay, the incompleteness of the

social revolution, the imperfection of war, and the unfulfilled hope of
children:

> As a child holds a pet
> Arms clutching but with hands that do not join
>
> . . . .
>
> So the earth-and-rock flesh arms of this harbour
> Embrace but do not enclose the sea.
>
> *(SC, 71)*

The persona symbolically tries to bring the diverse parts of incompleteness together and find the truth: "My circling arms rest on a newspaper
/ Empty in my mind as the glittering stone / Because I search for an
image" (*SC,* 71). But then nothing is complete in the waste and chaos
of war, and the poet, after the port is evacuated, "is left alone on the
bridge / Where the cleaving river trickles like saliva / At the exact
centre, solitary as a target" (*SC,* 72). "Port Bou" is one of Spender's
most accessible and powerful poems. The poet stands there, almost
asking to be wounded. He cannot actively participate in the cause, but
through his poetic sensibility he can express the suffering, the folly,
and the pity. That is some service after all. That is the purpose of the
Spanish Civil War poems.

Hugh D. Ford notes that instead of descanting on "fundamental
ideas about freedom and liberty," Spender's "poems expound upon
death, suffering, fear and concern over the fate of the innocent and the
cowardly."[34] In the Spanish Civil War poems, Spender ceased to try to
fuse poetry and public policy. The poems are without villains. The
subjects are the dead, the defeated, and the frightened. Spender's good
friend and coeditor of *Horizon,* Cyril Connolly, authored a colossal
understatement when he referred to "Mr Spender's not very martial
muse."[35] As Katherine Bail Hoskins says, "No absolute pacifist wrote
more convincing antiwar poems during the thirties than this fervent
apologist for collective security."[36]

Part Four of *The Still Centre* disappoints somewhat after the intensity
of Part Three, but its contents logically follow Spender's retreat from
political commitment. These poems seek primarily, but not exclu-
sively, to deal with the inanition and breakdown of Spender's first
marriage and the resulting loss, isolation, and disappointment with
love. Significantly and sadly, Spender dedicated *The Still Centre* to the
wife he was losing.

The poems of loss of love begin with "The Human Situation," wherein the persona's troubled past is exorcised by Eros and "my Womanly companion, / Revolving around me with light" (*SC*, 80). "The Separation" is a poem in which lovers are parted because the persona has been busy traveling, but unlike "The Human Situation," it falls back on clichés such as "my map / With meaningless names of places" (*SC*, 84). The lament is prosy:

> To bring me back to you, the earth
> Must turn, the aeroplane
> Must fly across the glittering spaces,
> The clocks must run, the scenery change
> From mountains into town.
>
>   (*SC*, 84)

But then comes the last stanza of the poem, which is strong Spender. The lovers will find peace together when the will to serve the outside world is curbed:

> Shuttered by dark at the still centre
> Of the world's circular terror,
> O tender birth of life and mirror
> Of lips, where love at last finds peace
> Released from the will's error.
>
>   (*SC*, 85)

"Two Kisses" and "The Little Coat" are two more love poems. The former has the longing persona remembering the kiss he wears "like a feather / Laid upon my cheek" (*SC*, 86), and the latter presents an extended metaphor in which a torn coat presages loss "like dolls in attics / When the children have grown and ceased to play" (*SC*, 87). The persona desires to be held in a "solemn kiss" that will provide "the loving stillness" (*SC*, 88).

"Variations on My Life: The First" and "Variations on My Life: The Second," the last love poems in the collection, are enigmatic pieces in which the tormented persona, with never enough air, space, or light, laments love past and lost, but realizes he will never abandon loving, "which nothing does refuse / and only death denies" (*SC*, 92).

In "The Mask," Spender again employs glass and reflection imagery as the persona sees "the world with lenses." The eyes are the windows on reality: "My life confronts my life with eyes" (*SC*, 101). Other people revolve around the circles of his sight, but their passions are invisible. "They are the mirrors of the foreign masks / Stamped into shapes" (*SC,* 102). We can only know people one at a time, and then, because of masks, only imperfectly, for reality is merely our own consciousness. Thus, the solipsism of "The Mask" is the perfect paradigm of modernity.

"Napoleon in 1814" is the longest (114 lines) poem in *The Still Centre* and clearly the product of prolonged and troubled political thought. Napoleon represents Stalin, who in the 1930s was "the Man of Destiny": "Men spoke of you as Nature, and they made / a science of your moods" (*SC,* 97). Was ever the idea of dictator encapsulated in so few words? Napoleon is presented in what Valentine Cunningham calls "heroic '30s images," such as "In you the Caesars," "sun," and "a superhuman shadow."[37] Spender was seeking to express the essence of a Napoleon. He had changed his mind about power politics and the morality of "good" tyranny fighting evil tyranny (i.e., Stalin versus Hitler). As in "The Mask," individual consciousness shapes Napoleon's self-image as "the genius whom all envied," but with a difference:

> You were the last to see what they all saw
> That you, the blinding one, were now the blind
> The Man of Destiny, ill destined.
>
> For, as your face grew older, there hung a lag
> Like a double chin in your mind. The jaw
> Had in its always forward thrust
> Grown heavy.
>
> (SC, 96)

Napoleon should have truly studied and understood himself. Instead, he was left with the "wreck of deeds, the empty words." And after all, what is history but words? Great rhetoric, now like Hitler's and Stalin's, is "hidden in the hollow bones." "Napoleon in 1814" is a fine example of how Spender could bring his knowledge of history, his admiration for greatness and strength, his distrust of military force, and his puissant imagery of war and death to bear on an issue of the gravest importance: the attraction and the peril of the cult of personality.

"To a Spanish Poet (for Manuel Altolaguirre)" is the last poem in *The Still Centre.* It is an *ave atque vale* to all that the "idea" of Spain connoted in the 1930s, to the decade itself, and to the poet's youth. An English poet eulogizes a Spanish poet who was driven from Spain by the fascists at the very end (*WW*, 238–39). Spender employs the key image of *The Still Centre* in "To a Spanish Poet"—the glass mirror—as he has the Spaniard stand absurdly in the ruins of his bombed home:

> Everything in the room was shattered;
> Only you remained whole
> In frozen wonder, as though you stared
> At your image in the broken mirror
> Where it had always been silverly carried.
>
> (*SC*, 105)

Both Spender and Altolaguirre have "stared out the window on the emptiness of a world exploding." Spender reminds us of the individual's powerlessness in the face of the egotism of states that create "these comedies of falling stone" (*SC*, 106). Spender is so moved by the suffering of Altolaguirre and his compatriots that he reaches back into his cultural heritage to employ Jacobean imagery by way of Eliot:

> Unbroken heart,
> You stare through my revolving bones
> On the transparent rim of the dissolving world
> Where all my side is opened
> With ribs drawn back like springs to let you enter
> And replace my heart that is more living and more
>   cold.
>
> (*SC*, 107)

Yet the poem ends on a note of hope. The song goes on. It may be night but the stars still shine:

> With your voice that still rejoices
> In the centre of its night,
> As, buried in this night,
> The stars burn with their brilliant light.
>
> (*SC*, 107)

I have left the first poem in Part Four, "Darkness And Light," until last because, like "The Uncreating Chaos," it is a crucial piece in the poet's struggle "to break out of the chaos of my darkness / Into a lucid day" (*SC*, 77). His words have become "eyes in night" trying "to reach a centre for their light" (*SC*, 77). He must find a place in the center of his will, but also, somehow, in the center of life and society. Paradoxically, the poet's conflicting postulates meet an artistic requirement: to have distant vision, to seek perspective, to stand aside and witness. He must stand "on a circumference to avoid the centre." Thus the dilemma that "centre and circumference are both my weakness" (*SC,* 77). Spender has located the source of modern artistic and intellectual paresis.

Finally, the persona in *The Still Centre* reveals the ambivalence and anxiety that foment modernism. The poet seeks strength of will to become a person of truth and integrity, and yet he knows, and reminds us, that human weakness is ever present, creating an inertia that leads to dangerous illusions. The "still centre" symbolizes that quiet, eternal place "from which the poet can stabilize his values and then come to terms with his world."[38] He has returned to the "edge of being." It is not surprising that Spender chose "Darkness and Light" as the epigram for *World within World.* How better could he summarize and preface the Manichaean conflict between freedom and determinism that structured the first half of his life?

Selected Poems

At just past the age of 30 Stephen Spender was internationally recognized as a major English poet. Faber and Faber, in an effort to bring to mass popular attention the works of the most significant contemporary poets, launched a series, rather ingenuously named Sesame Books, and Spender's *Selected Poems* (1940) appeared therein, as did books of Eliot, Auden, MacNeice, and others. *Selected Poems* contains 12 poems from *Poems,* 19 from *The Still Centre,* and selections from each of the five acts of the verse play *Trial of a Judge.*

During World War II, British poetry quite understandably went into a tailspin. All the poets, even those who had emigrated, were traumatized by the desperate struggle. Many magazines were suspended. Book publishing was curtailed. Most writers did various kinds of war service. Thus, Spender and his contemporaries held their relative positions during the conflict. With Auden in America and in disgrace with the general public, if not with his friends, the publication of *Selected Poems* authenticated Spender in Britain as the premier poet of the younger generation growing just a little long in the tooth. He was considered a spokesperson and a visionary striving to integrate self and society. Slowly but inexorably, Spender would slip from his justly held position of eminence through several collections of successively diminishing promise, until the public perceived him not as a fine poet but as that valuable but lesser contributor to culture, the essaying critic.

Chapter Three
Exile from Single Being: Later Verse

"Of human activities, writing poetry is one of the least revolutionary," Spender wrote in his 1933 essay "Poetry and Revolution."[1] He then went on for a decade to write radical political poetry supporting the Viennese Socialist revolt and the cause of the Left in Spain. "The poet, often a potential revolutionary, is able to escape the urgent problems of social reconstruction into a world of his own making," Spender wrote. "This world is a world of the imagination only bounded by the limits of imagination" (*NC*, 64). Spender opted for that escape clause in the 1940s, having found the circumferential place of distant perspective.

World War II was part of it. The war became a paradigm of human contempt for human life. Spender says in *Poetry since 1939* that he and other poets wondered "whether the war, which was certainly against Fascism, was for a purified cause."[2] Therefore, he turned to "introspective poems in search of universal experience through subjective contemplation" (*PS39*, 34). He was affected by what John Press calls "the 1940s . . . deliberate reaction against the previous decade."[3] Nonproletarian poets, notably Edith Sitwell, Robert Graves, and Dylan Thomas, were attracting greater critical attention and public interest. But very little British poetry written during the war or the years immediately following, a period of continued rationing and shortages, reconstruction, and the empire's disintegration, has proved enduring. Spender, like others, retreated into a self-sufficient poetic world of truth and peace, while paradoxically he became more and more a public figure. Thereafter, the subjects of his poetry change little: love, self, the horrors of war, pity, and personal sorrow. His propagandistic vein exhausted itself. His output slowed. The early tendency to write hastily and sometimes stumble on clichés passed. His imagery remained forceful and precise. But the energy waned, and seemingly, his confidence began to slip. Spender went on the defensive as the attrition of time and diminishing will wore down his inspiration and dispersed his audience.

Of course, during the war Spender wrote about the war, but he wrote not as a "war poet" but as a poet writing from a removed perspective. His struggle was with despair more than with the Germans, for he saw that human cruelty knows no bounds and no nation monopolized it. As a romantic poet, he needed inner isolation, but the price for that isolation in wartime was costly to his psychological equilibrium. Like most humanists, Spender had hoped and believed that progressive humanism would provide moral structure in an era of growing religious skepticism, but it had not. How could art or intellect solve the overwhelming problems of reality? The war was the mad triumph of irrationality and barbarism.

On the positive side, Spender's sexual discomfort had subsided and his feelings of betrayal and abandonment at the loss of his first wife were assuaged by a successful second marriage. Ironically, the conflux of humanist despair and emotional peace was not especially conducive to the production of poetry.

Ruins and Visions

Ruins and Visions (1942) contains 28 poems divided into four parts: the first three parts, "A Separation," "Ironies of War," and "Deaths," constitute the "ruins," and Part Four, the "Visions." The first three parts depict personal, political, and universal disintegration, and the last projects a path out of the ruins. Essentially, the poet is trying to comprehend the complex web of relationships that confuse and overwhelm him and, indeed, all of us.

The poems of "A Separation," which express grief over a woman loved and lost, are very personal, almost painfully so. The poet despairs of his art ever being capable of diverting the force and direction of immutable reality. The section opens with "Song," a heartbreaking, sardonic exposure of love betrayed and suffering endured. It is the kind of poem that caused Auden to say that it was Spender's capacity for humiliation that made him a poet. Here the poet berates, but still is able to understand, the friend who has stolen his love:

> Stranger, you who hide my love
> In the curved cheek of a smile
> And sleep with her upon a tongue
> Of soft lies which beguile,
>   Your paradisal ecstasy
> Is justified is justified

By hunger of all beasts beneath
  The overhanging cloud,
    Who, to snatch quick pleasures run,
    Before their momentary sun
  Be eclipsed by death.[4]

The persona is more angry with the woman who has left him, who (in his mind at least) is a person beyond trust, easily tempted by the novel:

Lightly, lightly from my sleep
  She stole, our vows of dew to break,
Upon a day of melting rain
  Another love to take;
    Her happy happy perfidy
    Was justified was justified
Since compulsive needs of sense
  Clamour to be satisfied
    And she was never one to miss
    The plausible happiness
Of a new experience.

                        (*RV,* 11)

The ironically titled "Song" is an example of the emotional openness in Spender, a quality that provoked compliments from, among others, David Daiches: "His verse has a smoothness, a limped quality, that distinguishes it from that of his contemporaries."[5] In that it is a direct and memorable expression of a poet's deep mental and emotional experience, "Song" is an exemplar of romantic poetry.

"A Separation" indicates that there is no remedy for a lost love that cannot be forgotten. The persona is unable to accept the "stumbling stumps of consolations" (*RV,* 13), an awkward phrase for an unpleasant condition. The theme of pity, so important in much of Spender's best poetry, degenerates into self-pity here and in the sonnet "The Vase of Tears," where we find "tears pouring from this face of stone" (*RV,* 14), and in "The Journey," where "our harsh tongues of to-day would run in tears" (*RV,* 17). It is not well that the persona calls his heart "a glass vase." The metaphor does not have a credible analogical basis. Having cotranslated Rainer Maria Rilke's *Duino Elegies* (1939), Spender was trying to compete with his German model in profundity and symbolism. It was a mistake, for as Geoffrey Thurley points out, he strained to find "analogical correlates for phenomena which do not especially seem

to have struck him, and his own natural metaphorical animism gives
way to an increasingly literary symbolism."[6]

"The Double Shame" is a self-accusing piece:

> At first you did not love enough
> And afterwards you loved too much
> And you lack the confidence to choose
> And you have only yourself to blame.
>
> (RV, 16)

The poem illustrates Spender's strengths and weaknesses at the time. A
soft center, hyperbole, failed metaphor, and symbols without clear
referents mar it: "Pull down the blind and lie on the bed / And clasp the
hour in the glass of one room / Against your mouth like a crystal doom"
(RV, 15). Yet Spender can hit upon the apt metaphor, as in this excellent image of lost love: "And each empty dress cuts out an image / In
fur and evening and summer and gold / Of her who was different in
each" (RV, 15). Still, the poem waivers tonally between pathos and
satire of love's agonies. In the end, it seems somewhat tactless.

"A Hall of Mirrors" employs the iterative mirror-glass images so
common in Spender's poetry. Entering "a hall of many mirrors," the
persona is

> Searching for that one face
> Of innocence: amongst your many faces
> Endlessly repeated in the empty spaces
> Of your own eyes;
> Suspended thinly on threads
> Of your own self-admiring gaze.
>
> (RV, 18)

But the face of innocence is lost and "truth . . . begs forgiveness" (RV,
19). The poem's weakness lies in a technique of Spender's at that time,
referred to by Louis MacNeice in *Modern Poetry* (1938) as "the parataxis
of early Chinese poets."[7] This stringing-together of disjointed images is
exemplified in these lines:

> Somewhere in the night, above the branches
> Restless with tongues of leaves over the square,
> Where you and I and all
> The false play-acting puppets are,
> In a high room, hidden in the darkness,

> There lies your heart, the truly good,
> Swathed in the flesh where all roses unfold.
>
> (*RV*, 19)

The persona admits that he and his ex-love are not heroes of myth nor archetypes of lost love. As in "No Orpheus, No Euridice" the persona and loved one are far from immortals. He may be searching everywhere, "looking and singing for his wife," but

> She has truly packed and gone
> To live with someone
> Else, in pleasures of the sun,
> Far from his kingdoms of despair
> Here, there, or anywhere.
>
> (*RV*, 22)

In "No Orpheus, No Euridice" and "A Wild Race," the last poem in "A Separation," Spender, the emotional autobiographer, attacks the excess of imagination that psychological stress engenders. The antiromantic positions of "A Wild Race" is based on the idea that for the poet it is ultimately the work that endures, not the pain. All lovers hurt each other and art is born of grief. If "the beloved, afraid, / Laughed and betrayed" (*RV*, 24), and the persona "never knew: that his heart / Was torn apart / By loss large as a vulture" (*RV*, 25), then time would know his suffering through his verse.

The poems in Part One are of mixed success. The pity is too personal. One might say there is too much falling on the thorns of life and too much bleeding. Also, the literary affectation, particularly in "The Vase of Tears" and "The Journey," distracts from the possibility of empathic communication. When Spender denounces affectation and self-pity in "The Double Shame," his work is more effective, and when he is direct, sarcastic, cool, and controlled, as in "Song," his work is as judicious as Juvenal's.

Part Two, "Ironies of War," is reminiscent of the third part of *The Still Centre,* but the word "ironies" indicates that there will be no glorification of a "righteous" cause here as there was of Republican Spain in the earlier work. In "The War God" the poet is seeking peace without retribution:

> Why cannot the one good
> Benevolent feasible

> Final dove descend?
> And the wheat be divided?
> And the soldiers sent home?
> And the barriers torn down?
> And the enemies forgiven?
> And there be no retribution?
>
> (RV, 29)

But hatred is interminably transmitted from generation to generation, and

> the conqueror
> Is an instrument of power,
> With merciless heart hammered
> Out of former fear,
> When to-day's vanquished
> Destroyed his noble father,
> Filling his cradle with anguish.
>
> (RV, 29)

Yet there is hope that hatred will disperse like oil befouling a self-cleansing sea. Spender is an idealist and believes in the future. Love can break the cycle of hate: "Though hidden under seas / Of chafing despair, / Love's need does not cease" (RV, 31). Here, however, infelicitous images, such as "their dead teeth bite the earth / With semen of new hatred" (RV, 30), detract once more.

"The War God" and "To Poets and Airmen" indicate that, like Marxist dialectic, Spender sees war as inevitable until a utopia of peace is established. "To Poets and Airmen" is dedicated to Michael Jones, an airman (WW, 266). Airmen require "a bullet's eye of courage / To fly through this age" (RV, 32) and in the desperate Battle of Britain. They are importuned:

> Before you throw away your childhood,
> With the lambs pasturing in flaxen hair,
> To plunge into this iron war,
> Remember for a flash the wild good
> Drunkenness where
> You abandoned future care,
> And then forget. Become what
> Things require.
>
> (RV, 32–33)

In an extended image of great beauty, "The Air Raid across the Bay" offers searchlights in the mythic sky:

> The shining ladders slant
> Up to the god of war
> Exalted on those golden stilts
> And riding in his car
> Of a destroying star.
>
> (*RV*, 35)

At the end of the raid, nature struggles back and survives "in an elemental magic / Of ripeness, which mocks / The nails through flesh torn" (*RV*, 35).

"Winter and Summer" transcends the cliché of winter as the season of despair and summer as the season of hope, as the persona hears "the groaning of the wasted lives." In deeply moving lines the poet affirms his hope and even belief that "furious volleys of charioteering power" will fade away:

> if my shadowed mind affirmed the light
> It would return to those green foolish years
> When to live seemed to stand knee-deep in flowers:
> There, winter was an indoor accident,
> Where, with head pressed against the glass, I watched
> The garden, falsified by snow,
> Waiting to melt, and become real again.
>
> (*RV*, 36–37)

"In Memoriam" rejects the humanistic optimism of "Winter and Summer" with a five-time-repeated refrain of war: "Where everything stops but the wishes that kill" (*RV*, 38). The "laughing lad Bill," who is a "fine feather-head," is questioned in death:

> Was your life, but a curveting arc of desire
> Ricochetting in flames on your own funeral pyre
>   Instinctive as birds,
> Where everything stops but the wishes that kill?
>
> (*RV*, 39)

The poem is less a lament for the death of an airman than for the loss of civilized values caused by war, as humans, "driven by intolerance, . . .

melt down the whirring bodies of boys / And their laughter distil / To plough metal hatred through the skies" (RV, 38). Perhaps the greatest evil of war is what it does to the human heart, inuring it to the fiercest cruelties.

The desire for peace reaches a crescendo in the most acclaimed poem in *Ruins and Visions,* "June 1940," that most despair-filled month of the war for the British, when the army was driven from Dunkirk and France fell. In the poem two old men, perhaps veterans of World War I, announce that "our minds must harden" (RV, 41). The poem mocks their patriotism and the attitude that in the end "of course, we shall win" (RV, 42). Win what? It was brave of Spender to have published "June 1940" in wartime, for its message is that "victory and defeat, both the same, / Hollow masks worn by shame" (RV, 42–43). Spender had given up supporting any system with poetry, because all systems resort to barbarism and use the gullible to slay the innocent, making war on life itself.

In Part Three, "Deaths," Spender is less self-obsessed than in Part One, even though he is describing failures, struggles, and sufferings, including the archetypal Oedipal battle between father and son and the wasting cancer of his beloved sister-in-law Margaret Spender. In "The Ambitious Son," Spender tries to placate and finally bury the ghost of his father, a man who remained committed to the political process and social reform. Father and son had in effect competed for fame. Spender had become so egotistical that he searched the newspapers daily looking for his name. His father had searched for immortality too, but

> Soon you lay in your grave like a crumpled clown
> Eaten by worms, by quicklime forgotten,
> Fake, untragic, pelted down
> By a generation still more rotten.
>
> (RV, 48)

However, the poet finds that he cannot totally forsake his father's vision, when "the prisoners and the homeless make me burn / With homesickness when I pass" (RV, 49). No father ever fully leaves his son. The poem is so nostalgic that it even brings back Spender's old images of machinery: "How like an engine do I press / Toward the terminus of my last breath" (RV, 49). Shades of "The Express"! Of course, the terminus now is not high art but death.

"The Drowned" is a maudlin poem memorializing sailors who died in the war at sea. We are not surprised to learn that "no letter reaches wrecks; / Corpses have no telephone" (*RV*, 53). "Tod und das Maed-chen" (Death and the Girl), the title from Matthias Claudius and Franz Schubert, and "Wings of the Dove," also the title of Henry James's 1902 novel about a dying woman, appear again, slightly altered and retitled as part of "Elegy for Margaret" in *Poems of Dedication* (1947). They treat poor Margaret Spender's agonized decline. She was to die three years after the publication of *Ruins and Visions.* "Tod und das Maedchen" vividly depicts her suffering:

> Where you are lying,
> The strong tide of your limbs drawn back
> By green tides of regret,
> And the sorrowful golden flesh
> Scorched on by disease,
> How difficult is dying
> In your living dying eyes.
>
> > (*RV*, 51)

The poet is tormented in "Wings of the Dove" because his sorrow can not help her:

> It does not carry a surgeon's knife
> To cut the wrongly multiplying cells
> At the root of your life.
> It can only prove
> That extreme love
> Stretches beyond the flesh to hideous bone
> Howling in the dark alone.
>
> > (*RV*, 56)

Margaret's suffering is symbolic of all the suffering in the raging war, but, finally, suffering is both individual and bipartite: there is the sufferer and there are those close ones who suffer vicariously because they love the bearers of the pain. Yet the poet's grief is only "thought, a dream," the "granite facts" are in the bed.

"The Fates," the last poem in Part Three, "Deaths," is the longest in *Ruins and Visions,* 155 lines divided into three sections. In the first, as he is wont to do, Spender presents life as theater. The "actors act the ritual of their parts / Clowns, killers, lovers, captains" (*RV*, 57), and the audience watches, hoping that the catastrophe will not envelop it, but, of course, it does, for "which are the actors, which the audience?" (*RV*, 58). The poet scorns the self-deceivers who ignore reality, like the aristocratic mother in the second and third sections who raised her son in an atmosphere of isolation from the "poverty, adultery, disease" that surrounded their comfortable world, only to lose him on "a field abroad," where he finds the truth at last:

> A whip of lead
> Strikes a stain of blood from his pure forehead.
> Into the dust he falls,
> The virginal face carved from a mother's kisses
> As though from sensitive ivory,
> Staring up at the sun, the eyes at last made open.
> (RV, 63)

Fate is terribly fierce to those who hide from truth. It is like a house cat turned into Blake's tiger: "As though the cat had turned into a tiger / Leaping out of a world become a jungle / To destroy its master" (RV, 62). Thus, the catastrophe is reserved for those who attempt to avoid seeing the tragedy of war. "The Fates" is the finale of "Ruins."

Part Four, "Visions," growns from the ruins that have preceded it; it sorts out the disasters and seeks, along a personal path, the poet's self-identity. He must find in lover and friend a familiar landscape, and "Visions" details the search for it.

"At Night" describes how darkness, like a drug, can ease the pressures of the real, presenting the persona, the "I" alone and naked, as "the image of his own loneliness" (RV, 68). "Dusk," several poems nearer to the final "To Natasha," is less dark. Serenity and old verities prevail. It is as if Spender yearned to reverse time, to be a Georgian poet like John Masefield, searching for the core of beauty:

> On earth below
> The knotted hands
> Lay down their tasks,
> And the wooden handles
> Of steel implements
> Gently touch the ground.
> The shifting animals
> Wrinkle their muzzles
> At the sweet passing peace,
> Like bells, of the breeze;
> And the will of Man
> Floats loose, released.
> (RV, 79–80)

"Daybreak" is a bright love sonnet, immediately preceding "To Natasha." The word "darling" from the beloved's lips "fell, from a dawn of fountains," upon his heart like "the song of the first bird" (*RV*, 82). Ruins are far from the persona's mind in this love lyric, the only one in the collection. Love for a woman consumes all fears, ambitions, and misgivings.

"The Barn" and "In a Garden" are tranquil pieces indicating a retreat to Wordsworthian contemplation. Like a nineteenth-century romantic, Spender, in "The Barn," builds a mood with a houseful of sensual, descriptive images. The poem is atypically nondidactic, a beautiful sound "hushed by whispers of leaves, and bird song" (*RV*, 70). And in "In a Garden" the persona is challenged to make poetry of nature:

> Had I pen ink and paper,
> I think that they could carry
> The weight of all these roses,
> These rocks and massive trees.
> (*RV*, 72)

In "A Childhood" the persona has met a girl "on the edge / Of your barbarous childhood" (*RV*, 73). He prays that with maturation "you may have the strength to become you" (*RV*, 74). In "Into Life" the beloved "never quite will learn / To see your life as whole, / Your mirrors are too blind" (*RV*, 75), but she may learn the truth that "what you were, you are, / And what you will be, you are, too (*RV*, 76). In "The Coast" the poet concludes that goodness continues to exist in the world: "Some acts of kindness wave their handkerchiefs," and joy may come from "flesh and bone" (*RV*, 78).

"To Natasha" ends *Ruins and Visions*. Spender had married Natasha Litvin in 1941. "Separation" ceased. He had found a love that would endure the seasons. Natasha is the final vision. Like Yeats, Spender can believe in order only after there has been disorder. It is the path and the proof. Second marriage brought closure to an open arc, although the future is always unchartable:

> Darling, this kiss of great serenity
> Has cast no sheet anchor of security
> But balances upon the faith that lies
> In the timeless loving of your eyes
> Our terrible peace, where all that was

> Certain and stated, falls apart
> Into original meanings, and the words
> That weighed like boulders on us from the past
> Are displaced by an earthquake of the heart.
>   (RV, 84)

The finest poems in *Ruins and Visions* are in Part Two, "Ironies of War." Although the quality of the work in general evidences a slight falling off from *The Still Centre,* Spender's poetic ability and energy remain strong. Most of the poems in the collection are compressed and consistent, but some are soft in theme or execution. Spender takes chances and reveals himself in the best tradition of romantic poetry. His gifted personality emerges undaunted from the ruins of war and the battles of life. Life and death, love and war, betrayal and forgiveness, suffering and salvation, separation and union, and the existential being become the elements of the Spender cosmos.

Poems of Dedication

Although some of its poems were composed late in the conflict, *Poems of Dedication* (1947) is essentially a product of the postwar era. Battle and politics have all but disappeared from the poems, and the personal, both tragic and joyous, has taken over. The collection is Spender's most intimate attempt to engage human consciousness, existence, love, and death. His approach to life grows even more positive because love is now the central factor in existence. *Poems of Dedication* contains 24 poems divided into four parts. Part One, "Elegy for Margaret," is a 6-poem lament for the author's sister-in-law, who died of cancer on Christmas Day, 1945. Part Two, "Love, Birth, and Absence," is dedicated "to Natasha." Part Three, "Spiritual Exploration," is dedicated to Cecil Day Lewis, and Part Four, "Seascape and Landscape," has a poem dedicated to Edith Sitwell.

Two poems in "Elegy for Margaret," "From a tree choked by ivy, rotted" and "Poor girl, inhabitant of a stark land" were previously published in *Ruins and Visions* as "Tod und das Maedchen" and "Wings of the Dove" (discussed above). The six poems demonstrate how the poet dealt with Margaret's death. His approach is platonic. The healthy hide in the dream of life, in which they unknowingly mimic the realities of the immortal, spiritual world. The poems are influenced by Rilke's *Duino Elegies,* which Spender had cotranslated in 1939 and which he later said "were the work of the perpetual transformation of beloved and tangible things into the invisible vibrations and excitability of our nature, which introduces new 'frequencies' into the pulsing fields of the universe."[8] In a sense, the *Elegies* chronicle Margaret's translation into the cosmos.

In "Darling of our hearts, drowning" the poet immediately engages the devastating fact of terminal illness: "The invisible vulture feeds on your flesh."[9] But death is more important than life if one believes in a spiritual world, and therefore death is also more important than love, so the poet will "wear your death / Next to my heart, where others wear their love" (*PD*, 12).

In "Dearest and nearest brother," Spender speaks to his grieving brother Humphrey to comfort him with the serene assertion that the sting of death can be assuaged by its meaning: it is a beginning, a confirmation, a marriage.

> As she will live who, candle-lit,
> Floats upon her final breath,
>
> . . . .
>
> Wearing not like destruction, but
> Like a white dress, her death.
>
> (*PD*, 14–15)

Margaret is merging, as all must do one day, with nature in "Already you are beginning to become." Her body will be a "fallen treetrunk with sun-burnished limbs / In an infinite landscape" (*PD*, 20). Spender metamorphoses the dying Margaret, "partly ghost," into that piece of earth she shall become. "The final act of love" fully and finally unfolds death eroticism in the "Elegy." In the Victorian manner, grief is visualized as a "deprived fanatic lover, / Naked in the desert" (*PD*, 22). Death is a visitor who becomes a lover. The lovers "assume this coarseness / Of loved and loving bone / Where all are all and all alone" (*PD*, 23). Death bonds us forever in the love of the universe. It is oneness and perfectibility.

"Elegy for Margaret" has a literary pedigree running from Theocritus down through the great elegies of English literature—Donne's elegies, Milton's "Lycidas," Dryden's "Mr. Oldham," Shelley's "Adonais," and Tennyson's "In Memoriam"—all of which are faintly echoed in Spender's carefully studied composition. Yet "Elegy for Margaret" was probably Spender's most emotionally exhausting work, a profound spiritual opportunity. It is also one of his most beautiful extended poems. The solace of art for the loss of a loved one has seldom been better presented.

The poems of Part Two, "Love, Birth, and Absence," deal with the joy of love's union and with recollections of ecstatic moments. The poems are resplendent with romantic imagery. "Summer" ostensibly glorifies the season, but really declaims the charms of a lover:

> The midsummer glow
> Reflected in her eyes
> Is colour of clover
> In grass flesh where she lies.
> Bird-shadow cloud-shadow
> Draw a net of sighs
> Over her from her sun-gold lover.
> (*PD*, 27)

"Four Eyes," two for each lover, see "the light / of world" and try unsuccessfully to be "a mesh / To net the summer hours" (*PD*, 28). The lovers are "locked / Within the lens of their embrace" in "The Dream" (*PD*, 29) as Spender continues his iterative and architectonic sight imagery. The lovers' passion produces a child "between their bodies rocked" (*PD*, 29). Natasha and Stephen's first child was born in 1945. the six-line "Man and Woman" sees love between them as an ennobling force in the universe. They "naked new life fashion" (*PD*, 30).

In "The Trance" the momentary separation of the persona and his lover in sleep proves his philosophy of the transcendence of love over the physical: "Our bodies, stripped of clothes that seem, / And our souls, stripped of beauty's mesh, / Meet our true selves, their charms outwitted" (*PD*, 31). The bed is also where the angel and the devil in lovers meet: "Our angel with our devil meets / In the atrocious night" (*PD*, 31–32). But there is accommodation, forgiveness, and understanding until "love's deep miracle" proves that physical union only prefigures true spiritual union.

"Absence" and "Lost" are poems about the pain and anguish of separation from a loved one. "Absence has the quality of ice / On a high peak" (*PD*, 33). The trouble between lovers vanishes upon their reunion when the persona see "the pure you in your eyes" (*PD*, 33). The persona can feel lost and sad in the house his wife and child have vacated. The room where he saw the mother "watching a child starred in his nakedness" is the precious place where their eyes collect "the light which each from each reflects" (*PD*, 35). His "seeing unseen eyes" will bring his thoughts "back to that one room where life was life most" (*PD*, 35).

Spender describes Part Three, "Spiritual Explorations," as "a parallel attempt to penetrate the very nature of human existence" (*PS39*, 37). It is the most philosophically profound section of *Poems of Departure*. He wants to examine the question of whether there is a meaning to human life, and he seeks a device with which to pursue that question. The structure of "Spiritual Explorations" is precise: a six-line prologue, seven sonnets, and a long free-form eighth section.

The prologue flags the points of exploration: observing the world and the cosmos, and recognizing that the cosmos is indifferent to human life. The stars speak only "a language of mirrors" (*PD*, 39). The sonnets are solid, formal vessels holding the heavy wine of speculation. The first focuses on human vulnerabilities: nakedness, hollow minds, "paper skulls." We play the game of meaningfulness in life, but soon "the multitudinous loneliness of death" will cure us of our illusions. Sonnet II repeats the existential terror, reading like the synopsis of a Beckett play:

> You were born; must die; were loved; must love;
> Born naked; were clothed; still naked walk
> Under your clothes. Under your skin you move
> Naked: naked under acts and talk.
>
> (*PD*, 40)

And the sonnet ends with a *danse macabre:* "Harlequin skeleton, it / Strums on your gut such songs and merry dances / Of love, of loneliness, of life being death" (*PD*, 40).

Sonnet III tells us that our progress is in the effort "to narrow / The gap between the world shut in the eyes / And the receding world of light beyond" (*PD*, 41). Our relationship to the cosmos shifts in this poem. Now we are what we are and shall never be more. This is the understanding that is the goal of exploration. We may build a city of stone, but we mortals have no hold on it, for it serves only to prove our existence, "our breath, our death, our love" (*PD*, 41). In sonnet IV the poet reminds us again that mortals "have only / Bodies, and graves," and though we learn much in life, "knowledge and memory, are unfurled / Within each separate head" (*PD*, 42). Nevertheless, we grow more lonely until we shed the world.

In sonnet V, however, hope emerges in traditional Christian form:

> The immortal spirit is that single ghost
> Of all time, incarnate in one time,
> Which through our breathing skeletons must climb
> To be within our supple skin engrossed.
>
> (*PD*, 43)

But those who reject the Holy Spirit and repel humanity are lost: "Shut in himself, each blind, beaked subject kills / His neighbour and himself, and shuts out pity / For that one winging spirit which fulfils" (*PD*, 43).

In sonnets VI and VII the first-person voice now appears, as the persona steps in to assert his truth: "I am that witness through whom the whole / Knows it exists" (*PD*, 44). His knowledge then gives meaning to the universe. The world may have its objective physical existence, but, paradoxically "the stars outside / Glitter under my ribs. Being all, I am alone" (*PD*, 44). Furthermore, when he dies, "the things, the vision, still will be. / Upon this eye reflections of stars lie / And that which passes, passes away, is I" (*PD*, 44). Humans may be the measure of all things, but what does it matter if we are mortal? The knowledge of death makes the persona sigh with sadness as he sees "mirrored in my consciousness, the ill / Chameleonic harlequin who'll die" (*PD*, 45).

Sonnet VIII seems extraneous. Spender omitted it and VII from *Collected Poems, 1928–1953*. In *Selected Poems* (1964) he included only I, III, and VI, slightly altered. Part Eight is also repetitious, as it calls for the unbandaging of eyes to reveal to someone "him as he is" and "show him your own existence as you are" (*PD*, 46). Still, sonnet VIII summarizes "Spiritual Explorations." It presents a skeptic's response to the world catastrophes the persona has seen and endured, and the ratiocination brings him some way toward faith and hope. The persona is crying out for insight while weeping from the pain of existential loneliness. The parallel to "Elegy for Margaret" is clear. The "Elegy" is the response to a private tragedy endured; "Spiritual Explorations" is the response to the public tragedies of war, cruelty, suffering, and death.

Part Four, "Seascape and Landscape," contains three poems linked by a central idea: the desire for freedom from prisons, from authority, from the strictures of time, and from the distances that impede love. "Midsummer" creates a desire in the persona to listen "to a dynamo of summer that revolves / Generating what glistens" (*PD*, 51). But like all of us he is "tied on strips of time / Caged in minutes" and "shut without pity / In a clock eternity" (*PD, 52*).

"Seascape" shows how the sea has its moods and how destruction lurks beneath the calm. The beautiful sea drowns butterflies and ships. "There are some days the happy ocean lies / Like an unfingered harp, below the land," (*PD, 53*), when heroes have been "by sea engulfed, their coins and eyes / Twisted by the timeless waves' desires / . . . / While, above them, the harp assumes their sighs" (*PD, 54*). The sea is the symbolic ocean of eternity and of the unity of space, time, and eternity into which all energy flows and all matter merges.

"Meeting," a love poem in five parts, expresses the oneness of lovers who are separated by great distance. Their eyes "see with each other's eyes / Though half a world between us lies" (*PD, 58*). So powerful is their love that they are seemingly able to consummate it even when apart:

> When we sleep, our separate dreams
> Flow into each other's streams
> Wave over far wave slips
> Our lips melt into our lips.
> On my tongue your tongue
> Rustles with your song my song.
>
> (*PD, 58*)

They have grown so close spiritually that they seem to have one voice and their unity augers union after death.

The limpidity and excesses notwithstanding, *Poems of Dedication* is a creditable collection of verse. In "Elegy for Margaret" and "Spiritual Explorations," Spender deals with complex feelings and eternal questions. He sets for himself the high-minded task, perhaps impossibly difficult, of reconciling existential loneliness and the search for traditional faith—the elusive goal of mid-twentieth-century philosophy. Also, he tries to assuage psychological pain in others and to gloss love and joy in himself. His new world is personal and braver than the old one. The climaxes are emotional, not personal. As in the 1930s, Spender is here a man of his time, but the time is a lesser age.

The Edge of Being

Paradoxically, the 25 poems of *The Edge of Being* (1949) move Spender closer to positions of both faith and existentialism. Politics continues to decline as a subject, with the exception of "Returning to Vienna, 1947." Love is less central too. A philosophical poet emerges. The war is not over for Spender, however, and there is much guilt to expiate. The book is a sampler, the pieces discrete and ungrouped. Spender, who was 40 when the collection appeared, had matured considerably as both poet and person, and could look back on a body of work of high quality and sizable quantity. In *The Edge of Being,* Spender shows that he has eased into his natural voice. He has adopted the political, social, domestic, sexual, and religious attitudes that would serve him for the rest of his working life.

The first poem in *The Edge of Being,* "O Omega, Invocation," is a prayer to God, the Alpha and Omega. The letter O beginning the poem symbolizes the complete circle, the cycle of life, the unity of God. Also, O, as the last letter of the Greek alphabet, represents ending and zero, the final nothingness: "black / Hoop, circling on white / Paper, vanishes where the eye / Springs through thee, O."[10] All humans live, before eternity, on the edge of the O, the edge of being. The soul's progress in from the edge to, in Yeatsian terms, the unity of being.

"The Angel," "Madonna," and "Judas Iscariot" are poems with a traditional religious content. The persona in "The Angel" would have us withdraw from the world of sense and to join the unity of humanity, for "each is involved in the tears and blood of all" (*EB,* 27). Contentment and fulfillment come with the reduction of will and the acceptance of communion: "We have no inviolate instants where we are / Solid happiness hewn from day, set apart / From others afar" (*EB,* 27). Mortality is also shared. The angel warns us of the evil in rejecting God's charity and hope: "He is truth's own doom / Blowing news of evil on a golden trumpet" (*EB,* 27).

In "Madonna" the Virgin has a vision, while Christ is in her womb, of either a God-loving people or "heroes whose rays / Murder in the womb" (*EB,* 45). Her Son will later say to humankind, "Choose!"

"Judas Iscariot" is the most interesting of the religious poems in *The Edge of Being.* The dramatic monologue presents Judas as positing himself as an heroic victim. In a flowing, conversational tone Judas speaks as a spirit addressing the modern world as one with "the eyes of twenty centuries." He looks back to his life and is angered that he has been portrayed as the archetypal betrayer. Although he was not sinless, he argues that God, omnipotent and omniscient, is the true betrayer, for He is the First Cause:

> But who betrayed whom? O you,
> Whose light gaze forms the azure corridor
> Through which those other pouring eyes
> Arrow into me—answer! Who
> Betrayed whom? Who had foreseen
> All, from the first?
>
> .   .   .   .
>
> Who knew
> I must betray the truth, and made the lie
> Betray its truth in me?

> (*EB*, 16–17)

Those who denigrate Judas now, he argues, are hypocrites, the same kind of people who once mocked Jesus. The sad truth is that hypocrisy and persecution live on in humankind. "Judas Iscariot" is one of the most searching and profound poems in *The Edge of Being*.

Other dramatic monologues in *The Edge of Being* are "Faust's Song" and "Tom's A-Cold." In "Faust's Song" the power of love over knowledge in books is recognized by the scholar, who desires to be "reborn in the blonde landscape of a woman" and to die, in the Elizabethan sense, "in the river of eyes!" (*EB*, 15). In "Tom's A-Cold," Tom speaks in eighteenth-century rhymed couplets. Spender is successfully experimenting here with a form fresh for him. He proves that he can sustain a classical distance from his material. Tom is like Tom O'Bedlam (Edgar in disguise) in *King Lear*, but Spender's Tom is a man of the twentieth century who has come to realize that when the world is demented, madness is as viable a way of life as saneness. The new Tom once went "clothed in herringbone tweed" (*EB*, 37), but now he knows the true pain of the poor, bare, forked animal that is man. He understands "the sick botched lives, / The drink, the whoring and the knives" (*EB*, 41). In death,

> Where I lie in gravestone rhyme [like the poem],
> My eyes are these two pools which climb
> Through grey reflections to the sky—
> My world asking your world: "Why?"

> (*EB*, 42)

Why vanity, why passion, why struggle, why competition, when you know from the gravestones what the end is?

Besides "Faust's Song," the only love poems in *The Edge of Being* are

"O Night O Trembling Night," "Epithalamion," "Ice," and "Weep, Girl, Weep." "O Night O Trembling Night," like a troubador's ballad, evokes sexual love through Christian symbolism. The persona's "mouth was a vague animal cry / Pasturing on her flesh" (*EB*, 11). The loved one's body becomes the Host, and "her naked love, my great good news." The sexual act is the Gospel in this very erotic poem.

"Epithalamion" is a traditional wedding song, like Edmund Spenser's "Epithalamium" and Shelley's "Epithalamium" and "A Bridle Song." Spender informs the marrying couple that their unity is beyond time and space. It

> should be
> Stretched beyond this sheeted space
> Where curling limbs agree,
> Into a timeless bodiless grace
>   (*EB*, 46)

The poet blesses and wishes well. His final prayer: "O love, be indivisible!"

"Ice" is a sensual reminiscence of a winter's day when the persona's kiss brought fire to a woman's frozen face as "her smiling eyes / Shone with the health of the ice" (*EB*, 18). Hot-blooded poems like this and "Epithalamion" refute some present criticism of *The Edge of Being*, like A. T. Tolley's dismissal of the collection as a "depressingly lifeless book."[11]

"Word" is a little rhyme game. "Empty House" finds the persona missing his absent son when he tries to tidy up the boy's room. "Weep, Girl, Weep" is a poignant lament for a girl whose lover has been shot down and killed in war. Her sorrow "makes a great angel" (*EB*, 26). "Awakening" is a pessimistiic, unmoving poem in which "the whole sky opens to an O" and "the clocks grow beards" (*EB*, 14). "On the Third Day" is a poem of summer in which on successive days the persona lies in the valley enjoying the sensuous world and then climbs to the timberline, from which the world is obscured and where, in an unfortunate cliché, he "could not see the wood for the trees"; but on the third day, he "sprang from the forest / Into the wonder of a white snowtide" (*EB*, 12), where he finds perspective and spiritual renewal.

"Returning to Vienna, 1947" is a major work in *The Edge of Being*. Poets, like the rest of us, enjoy revisiting places of early challenges and first loves: "Vienna of my loving my first woman," Vienna where "the flower of my first flesh unfolded" (*EB,* 20). But, for Spender, Vienna was also where in 1934 the fascists killed "the small empiric saints" who were "shot down singing in their tenements" (*EB,* 21).

The poem is divided into seven parts (nine in the original version). Part I is a traditional invocation to the muse, "Femine Vienna," and in the central "Graben Square" the persona recalls the wars and plagues that have ravaged the city. Part II invites the reader to the haunts of the persona's love affair: the cafés in the city of music and the Vienna Woods. Parts III and IV, however, depict the ironic clash of passionate love and deadly politics: "Beyond the crystal bowl of our joined gaze—/ There was reality" (*EB,* 21), for there they saw the "burning bodies like the spokes / Of cartwheels thrown down" (*EB,* 21) and there they endured "the tears and bloodshot vein of seeing / The outer world destroy the inner world" (*EB,* 22). In Parts V and VI the city falls in "one instant of one night" (*EB,* 23). Statuary imagery, introduced in Part I, reaches a high point in VI as "the statued angel falls upon her knees" (*EB,* 23). Rubble and dust are everywhere. In Part VII the poet has come "back to the fallen dust" (*EB,* 24) in shame for not having fought on the side of the dead Socialist martyrs, for having lived over "the edge of being," and for not having loved enough too. He now knows that love is the mainspring of life. It "holds each moment to each moment / With architecture of continual passion" (*EB,* 25).

"Returning to Vienna, 1947" works well. It is more successful than its predecessor, *Vienna,* but then it is a much more modest endeavor. Here Spender properly balances the counterpointing themes of romantic passion and political struggle. He speaks with directness, clarity, and an authentic diction. He is no longer trying to be Eliot; he is Spender. But when *Vienna* had that never-reignitable fire of youth, when a sensitive young man knows how to hang his sympathies on the right hangers (the oppressed, the needy, the deserving, the human), when a young poet can take wild chances with poetry, people, and politics.

The Edge of Being contains six war poems, or, more precisely, postwar poems, for they are reflections in peacetime on the immediate violent past. "Epilogue to a Human Drama" powerfully evokes the bombing of London:

> The City burned with unsentimental dignity
> Of resigned wisdom: those stores and churches
> Which had glittered emptily in gold and silk,

> Stood near the crowning dome of the cathedral
> Like courtiers round the Royal Martyr.
>
> (*EB*, 28)

Here is a drama for the world's stage, with "heroes, maidens, fools, victims, a chorus" (*EB*, 28). Spender is at his descriptive and imagistic best as he masterfully transforms his experience as a fireman in the Blitz into the "tragedy" of London.

"Rejoice in the Abyss" is a poem of grim hope. Like "Epilogue to a Human Drama," it has as its subject an air raid on London. Waiting in fear for the raid to cease, the persona imagines "the photograph my skull might take / Through the eye sockets, in one flashlit instant" (*EB*, 30) when the walls of his house smash down on him. "But the pulsation passed, and glass lay round me" (*EB*, 30). The persona imagines that the streets "were filled with London prophets" who called out, "Rejoice in the abyss!" and denied meaning in individual life, for "each life feeds upon the grief of others" (*EB*, 31). We are always glad and guilty when calamity strikes others and we are spared. We must accept that life is only the abyss between birth and death.

"A Man-Made World" is a bleak poem arguing that humans have created this uncomfortable world, which pays us back in "money, steel, fire, stones, / Stripping flesh from bones." (*EB*, 33). Industrial human-kind has created a nightmare of machines and weapons. "Man-made toys" bring the "siren wails," and "while the gloom descends / . . . our means becomes our ends" (*EB*, 33). That end is loneliness, "with no saving star" (*EB*, 32).

"The Conscript" sees the ghost of previous armies and their skeletons. He cries out, "Father! Father! I come!" (*EB*, 34). "Almond Tree in a Bombed City" employs heavy enjambment to disguise a strictly rhymed and tightly structured poem:

> In the burned city, I see
> The almond flower, as though
> With great cathedral-fall
> Barbarian rage set free
> The angel of a fresco
> From a cloister wall.
>
> (*EB*, 35)

Although the city is burned, there is hope, heaven, and art—an "angel of Fra Angelico . . . To our world of ash will bring / Annunciation of Spring" (*EB*, 35). The persona is sure it will happen.

In "Responsibility: The Pilots Who Destroyed Germany, Spring, 1945," Spender declares his lasting guilt, which "turns thoughts over and over like a propeller" for having willed the bombing of a German town: "My will exploded. Tall buildings fell." Now the poet uses the past war as a subject for introspective writing: "I tie the ribbons torn down from those terraces / Around the most hidden image in my lines" (*EB*, 36). He is ashamed. The just person cannot justify war's murder, regardless of the provocations.

"Memento" is for the other face of Germany, not as victim of bombings but as perpetrator of one of history's greatest crimes: the Holocaust. In 10 lines Spender evokes the horror of the concentration camps filled with wretched humans whose "eyes sunk jellied in their holes/ Were held toward the sun like begging bowls" (*EB*, 48). Man's inhumanity to man shocks and perplexes the poet.

The last three poems in *The Edge of Being* are existential pieces. "Speaking to the Dead in the Language of the Dead" is a fine poem, a kind of *Rake's Progress* of a romantic poet, in a five-part narrative. Parts I and II show the reader his dissipation. Part III presents the relationship between his creative work and his destructive life. Part IV invites wonder as to how such a person could leave posterity "thoughts like footprints across snow." Part V offers the existential answers: "We live on a plane / Where our life is the blurred and jagged edge / Of all who ever died" (*EB*, 52). Moreover, we create the poet's values in our minds: "Through us you enter into your ideal" (*EB*, 53).

In "We Cannot Hold onto the World" the persona describes two deaths: an athlete who has been shot and a woman writer, perhaps Virginia Woolf, who has drowned herself. There are no meaningful explanations for such deaths. Life is random: "A turning wheel scatters / Stars upon the wind." It is hard for a poet to "regain / The concentrated mind / From blowing dust outside" (*EB*, 54). One cannot dwell on loneliness and emptiness and yet continue to work.

Spender's great concern for time passing and death brought him to "Time in Our Time." Existentialists believe that they can only be true to themselves if they accept the finality of death and live constantly with the thought of its approach. The persona acknowledges that he "was cast naked out of non-existence" and that he is "moving from inconceivable beginning / To inconceivable end." The self is "cadaver planing and spiralling through the dark" (*EB*, 55). It is the phenomenal instant that matters, and love "which penetrates through falling flesh" (*EB*, 56). Spender's absorption with the nature of time recalls a well-known passage in Eliot's "Burnt Norton": "Time present and time past / Are both perhaps present in time future, / And time future contained in time past."

It is clear in *The Edge of Being* that some of the passion, intensity, and commitment has drained from the poetry of Stephen Spender. At 40 the poet was not the idealist and visionary he had been at 20. His perception of life and his weltanschauung darkened, while his thoughts became more inward and personal. Yet Spender remained the romantic poet and his style continued clear and fluid. At their best, the poems of *The Edge of Being* are precise, often passionate, and frequently profound. They are not to be written off because they are different from what he had done previously and what others like W. H. Auden, Edith Sitwell, and Dylan Thomas were then doing.

Collected Poems, 1928–1953

Spender added only seven poems to his canon when he published his first *Collected Poems* (1955), a fact that would seem to indicate that he then thought of himself primarily as a thirties poet. Spender made few changes in his poems, mostly minor—"no more than a discreet and almost unnoticeable minimum of technical tidyings up."[12] To his credit, Spender did not attempt to tidy up or change his early political image from young Communist to young humanist by altering passages here and there in the 1930s poems.

The first new poems in *Collected Poems, 1928–1953* are three pieces about Spender's daughter: "To My Daughter," "Missing My Daughter," and "Nocturne." The first two show Spender's developing sensitivity to, and concern for, the very existence and the needs of other individual humans. Group interest fades. Spender now begins to focus on what G. S. Fraser calls "the shining transparency of the single vision."[13] "To My Daughter," only five lines long, defines the great and permanent love the poet has for his child. Her whole hand grasped his finger, and he will never forget that clutching grip: "All my life I'll feel a ring invisibly circle this bone with shining" (*CP* 1955, 186). The tone, diction, and imagery of the piece are near perfect.

In "Missing My Daughter," Spender employs conventional rose imagery to evoke the fragile beauty of his child, whom he misses as he sits at his desk trying to write: "This blank page stares at me like glass / Where stared-at roses wish to pass / Through petalling of my pen" (*CP* 1955, 187). It is amusing to contemplate a poet writing that he cannot write. The child enters and becomes a "white poem. / The roses raced around her name" (*CP* 1955, 188). Like "To My Daughter," "Missing My Daughter" is precision work, without a wasted word.

Written in the third person, "Nocturne" has two parents imaging that the cries in the night of their six-week-old daughter symbolizes the world's suffering, which they and others must strive to assuage, for they, like all humans, are capable of doing unspeakable things: "Parents like mountains watching above their child, / Envallied here beneath them, also hold / Upon the frozen heights, the will that sends / Destruction" (*CP* 1955, 190). The terrible weight of the world is upon parents and child, whose screams of "primal life" remind her parents that in the dark night of the soul there are "men's plots to murder children" and thus there is "no truth but that / Which reckons this child's tears an argument" (*CP* 1955, 191). There is also a gentle, humorous spin to this grave poem in the thought of young parents universalizing their guilt because their infant is crying.

Three new poems in *Collected Poems, 1928–1953* portray foreign landscapes. "In Attica" begins by describing a landscape, but then moves leisurely to a comment on how the gods have sculptured the land as the Greeks did their steles. Both gods and Greeks teach us immortality, "where the dying / Are changed to stone on a gesture of curved air, / Lingering in their infinite departure" (*CP* 1985, 181). "Messenger," addressed to the Greek poet George Seferis, describes a runner traversing Greece to a temple where he "kisses the white stone":

> He lifts his eyes where
> Grooved columns are quivers
> From which the archer sun
> Takes arrows to shoot
> Through his eye-sockets.
> (*CP* 1955, 183)

In the end, however, it is the poet who is the messenger and his message is that he exists. Ruined Europe has no message for ruined ancient Greece except to affirm the poet's "I am!" As long as the poet survives, beauty and history survive.

"Sirmione Peninsula," a poem of lost love, takes its title from an old Roman site in northern Italy. The persona has returned with a new love to the place he had visited with an earlier, still sorely missed lover. The new wife "seemed sad / Seeing me self-enclosed in my view of the view / That shut her out from me" (*CP* 1955, 192–93). The persona thus brings pain to his wife, but he cannot help himself. It is as if he were alone, "since she with whom I would be is not at my side, / With her hair blown back by the winds of the whole lake view, / Lips parted as though to greet the flight of a bird" (*CP* 1955, 193).

"Dylan Thomas," the last new poem in *Collected Poems, 1928–1953,* is an elegiac tribute to Spender's troublesome friend, who died in November 1953. Spender commemorates and captures the essence of "this roaring ranter, man and boy," the prolific poet whose "poems he shed out of his pockets" (*CP* 1955, 194). Spender presents Thomas as an effigy of Guy Fawkes set ablaze for popular entertaining but lighting up the sky as angels do. Spender was, and is, loyal to his friends to death and beyond. Thomas, like the poet in "The Messenger," has said "I am!" and Spender generously places him among the great.

The new poems in *Collected Poems, 1928–1953* continue the process of withdrawal from the political arena. Spender was struggling now to board, and grapple with, immediate moments and to explore the nature of time, consciousness, and the pain of mortality. The fewness of new poems included six years after his previous volume indicated a withdrawal from poetry as well as from politics.

Selected Poems

The *Selected Poems* of 1964 was first published in America and reprints only a few poems from the *Selected Poems* of 1940. All but three 1964 poems had been published before in various volumes. Alterations are few. Spender notes in his introduction that much of his recent work has been "tentatively written."[14]

"Subject: Object: Sentence" is one of Spender's most humorous poems, which of course is not saying a lot. It is clever but strained, a linguistic *tour de force* to be recommended to teachers of English grammar. The narrative of puns in a word game begins, "a subject thought: because he had a verb / With several objects, that he ruled a sentence" (*SP* 1964, 77). He is "*having's* slave" and means to "free himself from the verb *have*" because his "objects were *wine, women, fame* and *wealth.*" In the end, he realizes that language has tricked and betrayed him by means of a handbook full of teaching terms. Finally he understands: "A sentence is condemned to stay as stated—/ As in *life-sentence, death-sentence,* for example" (*SP* 1964, 77). Spender is saying that what is written remains written and one is fated to live out his or her sentence.

"Earth-Treading Stars That Make Dark Heaven Light" is abstract and complex. Again Spender opposes darkness and light. Now, however, a new truth is revealed, and it is made of flesh, for when we make love we see "into each other's night" and transcend to a fidelity that is like the "most brilliant star" (*SP* 1964, 79).

"One More New Botched Beginning," the last piece in the *Selected Poems* of 1964, is a poem of three memories: "Ten years ago here in Geneva, / I walked with Merleau-Ponty by the lake." Now the philosopher friend has died and the poet selfishly but humanly has reacted with the exclamation "I'm still living!" The the poet recalls seeing his son in Geneva, years before, as a child dancing "on one leg. Leaning forward, he became / A bird-boy" (*SP* 1964, 80). Then, in a great explosion of poetry, the persona vividly indicates the pressure and sweet pain of memory:

> Such pasts
> Are not diminished distances, perspective
> Vanishing points, but doors
> Burst open suddenly by gusts
> That seek to blow the heart out.
>   (*SP* 1964, 81)

In the third recollection Spender comes to the main theme of the poem: the existential randomness of life and the reality of the death of two poet friends. He envisions

> Three undergraduates standing talking in
> A college quad. They show each other poems—
> Louis MacNeice, Bernard Spencer, and I.
> Louis caught cold in the rain, Bernard fell
> From a train door.
>   (*SP* 1964, 81)

Finally, "their lives are now those poems" that identified them when they were living. Of course his "life" one day will be his poems, and he will join his friends back at Oxford where they "still stand talking in the quad" (*SP* 1964, 81). "One More New Botched Beginning" is a particularly fine poem and a precursor of the strong, fresh poems that would appear in the next volume of poetry.

The Generous Days

The Generous Days (1969), of which the second edition (1971) published by Faber in Britain and Random House in the United States, is

the fuller, definitive edition, contains 21 new poems and 8 epigram-
matic pieces under the rubric "Bagatelles." Spender also republished
"One More New Botched Beginning," of which he says in "Acknowl-
edgements and Note" that he included it "because it seemed to sum up
the mood of elegiac reminiscence of the poems that precede it in this
volume."[15] *The Generous Days* is a significant body of work. It appeared
after Spender's sixtieth birthday and was his first volume of new poetry
in 20 years.

Although the number of new poems is few after so long a wait, the
poetry in *The Generous Days* shows little falling-off in power, with
Spender grown more controlled, disciplined, laconic, and spare, unlike
his friend and foil Auden, who grew more relaxed, colloquial, and
diffuse with time. The superior poems in *The Generous Days* are those in
which Spender strives to create a union of the spirit and the flesh. The
unifying force is the consummation of passionate life by the acceptance
of death. In this last substantial collection of new work, the wisdom of
a full life is brought to bear on the use of memory and the nature of
existence.

The first poem in the volume, "If It Were Not," depicts a brooding
attitude toward the passing of time and then sets a tone for the collection. The poet sings of his love for the natural world, the individuality
of living things, the beauty and the blessings of wife and child in a
garden, how "clocks notch such instances / On time" and how the artist
chisels "memories / Within a shadowy room, / Transmuting gleams of
light to ships / Launched into a tomb" (*GD*, 12). The poem, a sharp
and poignant reminder of mortality, is typical late Spender—a poem of
icy beauty.

"Last Days," dedicated to John Lehmann, is the first of several reminiscences in *The Generous Days*. Lehmann, a poet and editor, was one of
Spender's oldest friends. Spender remarks on Lehmann's reach and
scope, as if they could embrace the entire globe, "Held in his arms, he
felt the earth spin round" (*GD*, 13). "V.W. (1941)" is a reconstruction
of "We Cannot Hold onto the World" in *The Edge of Being,* a eulogy for
Virginia Woolf, who along with her husband, Leonard, had helped
Spender in his early career. She is presented sadly as a "wild-eyed" artist
made mad by her own imagination and genius, until through suicide
her tormented mind grew "cold and silent as the stones" (*GD*, 19) with
which she weighted down her dress.

Two poems eulogize Spender's friend Peter Watson, the wealthy
patron and art editor of *Horizon* magazine. "On the Photograph of a

Friend, Dead" is an attempt to understand death in terms of memory and to resurrect a deceased friend's image through photography:

> To me, under my hand, in the Dark Room
> Laid in a bath of chemicals, your ghost
> Emerged gelatinously from that tomb;
> Looking-glass, soot-faced, values all reversed
> The shadows brilliant and the lights one gloom.
>
>   (*GD*, 24)

However the persona cannot reverse both the process of photography and his memory to recreate the person from the image. The photo "endlessly asks me: Is this all we have?" (*GD*, 24). The resurrection of the photo is not enough.

The second Watson poem, "Voice from a Skull," presents one nature symbol after another to infuse meaning in the Japanese fashion. An Oriental boat traverses the sea of life, and one man's existence is turned into a Japanese print. The voice from the poet's skull comes from the world within world.

Two more poems for old friends are "Four Sketches for Herbert Read," the poet-critic who died in 1968, and "To W. H. Auden on His Sixtieth Birthday," which Spender commemorated in 1967. "Four Sketches for Herbert Read" show Read as a youth in "Innocence" and as a World War I "Young Officer" watching his soldiers as if they were grazing sheep. "Conferencier" has the poet sketching his friend on the speaker's platform, and "Anarchist" locates the poet in France during the student rebellion of 1968, learning of Read's death. "To W. H. Auden on His Sixtieth Birthday" honors Spender's mentor, who, like his younger admirer, converted industrialism to poetry by "scrambling madly over scrap heaps / To fish out carburettors, sparking plugs" and "rigged such junk into new, strange machines." Spender still smarts over his older friend's critical barks directed at "the young Romantic": "Your words lobbed squibs / Into my solemn dream" (*GD*, 31). But the wound did "blossom to a rose," and after all, these are the generous days. Auden taught him hard but true lessons, and is here repaid with admiration and love.

"The Chalk Blue Butterfly" is image-impacted. Like a child observing, the persona dwells on the details of the beautiful insect: "Opening, shutting, on a hinge / Spring at touch of sun and shadow" (*GD*, 14). But the miraculous world of childhood and butterflies cannot be retained, and "today I am alone." The poet's son is the focus in "Boy, Cat, Canary," in which the persona, in his mature wisdom, hopes the lad does not see the ruins of Ilium in the naming of his bird, Hector. In "A Father in Time of War" the poet recalls taking his wife to the hospital to give birth to a "human phantom" (*GD*, 16) as the bombardment raged around them. In peace, the world, like "dizzy spinning tilting upside-down flags," is reborn. "The Child Falling Asleep in Time of War" floats on her boat-bed blessed by her father's kiss.

"Almond Tree by a Bombed Church" is dedicated to Spender's friend the sculptor Henry Moore. A "jewel-wing almond tree," nature's art, has grown through the tracery of a bombed church. Its "leaves and burning petals glow" (*GD*, 18) where a stained-glass angel once flourished. The almond tree, a symbol of long life, is also a rebirth of "luminous new life." "Mein Kind Kam Heim (after Stefan George)" is a ballad in which "my boy came home / The seawind still curves through his hair" (*GD*, 20), and the happy father rejoices in his son's return and maturation. "Sleepless" is an insomniac's poem, a debility suffered by many writers. The persona hears a strange noise and wonders if the house is falling apart and what bills he will now incur. Then he imagines "the walls / Crumbling away." Finally all that gloom reminds the persona that he too will "disintegrate / With the plaster—but . . . at a faster rate" (*GD*, 21). The lugubriously amusing poem turns mysterious as the persona thinks a noise is "that friend once / I shut him outside / Sink or swim—well, he sank," and like a guilt-born ghost he cries, "Let me in!" after "twenty years in the rain" (*GD*, 21). The poem indicates the significance of friendship in Spender's life and the degree to which he strove to be loyal.

The title poem, "The Generous Days," a four-part piece, is a poem of maturity, when one has come to "the generous days that balance / Soul and body" (*GD*, 22). It is a time to take up causes again, but it is also a time to cherish the mundane aspects of life and be "mindless of soul, so their two bodies meet." Of course the fierce, tough world will make sure that one day the persona will "be taken, stripped, strapped to a wheel." Worse, there is old age: "Then to himself he will seem loathed and strange" (*GD*, 23). Finally there is death. The poem's *carpe diem* message is delivered with great power and conviction.

"Fifteen-Line Sonnet in Four Parts," far from a traditional sonnet, is a metaphysical conundrum. The persona, talking to his lover, sees her "second you," after they make love. Time moves on, and "today, left only with a name, I rage, / Willing these lines—willing a name to be /

Flesh, on the blank unanswering page" (*GD,* 27). Articulation, the poet's craft, leads to frustration, because it cannot recreate a loved one gone. Another poem about love and writing is "What Love Poems Say," where again the persona looks back, fusing the writing of the poem with the memory of the experience. Thus, as in so many Spender poems, the subject is bifurcated into the experience and the process. The persona speculates, "It is as though I were / In all the universe the centre / Of a circumference" (*GD,* 28). This is the central iterative image of Spender's later poetry. The poet is surrounded by lights that have "eyes watchful, benevolent," representing cosmic history, humanity in general, and his audience specifically. Most important, however, the poet, conscious of artifice, notes that his lover is a product of language: "You come with a word." Through and in the process of poetry love binds time to a place and an action and, for a brief moment, holds the terrible universe at bay.

"Bagatelles" is a selection of 12 epigrams, epitaphs, observations, and dedications. The poem "Matter of Identity" finds the poet trying to understand whether anyone has an individual existence or is merely a piece of history: "He never felt quite certain / Even of certainties" (*GD,* 34). "To Become a Dumb Thing" consists of three word paintings, like illustrations on a Japanese scroll: harbor scenes and a conversation at a café, salted with a proliferation of asterisks.

The last two poems in *The Generous Days* are fun pieces. "Central Heating System" was written while Spender was teaching at the University of Connecticut at Storrs, and the central heating system kept him awake with its clanking. The noises were like the barking of watchdogs deterring "the ice-fanged killer" (*GD,* 42), New England cold. "Art Student" has the former young rebel of the 1930s confronting the young rebel of the 1960s who thinks that dumping offal from the slaughterhouse in a college exhibition is art. "Anyway, he thinks, / Art's finished" (*GD,* 43). But in the end the poet is sympathetic to the student's inarticulate attempt to "send people back / To the real thing—the stinking corpse" (*GD,* 44). The satire is effective and partially self-directed, for, after all, the young, sensitive, outraged Spender had once called for attention to the "real things" of his time.

The image of the poet emerging from *The Generous Days* is that of an artist who now, in advancing age, sees and portrays himself as a merchant of memories. The days have indeed been generous, and he is grateful. They have passed. On the whole, the poems of *The Generous Days* do not contain the passion, the power, and the energy of the earlier volumes, such as *The Still Centre,* that made Spender's name. Nevertheless, they are mainly profound, fresh, and original. One critic, Victor Howes, described them in 1971 as crystal clear in their imagery, resonant in their song, as fine as any lyric being written in the present.[16] *The Generous Days* indicates continual intellectual growth and artistic maturation. The poems are new wine in old bottles and are worthy of more attention than they have received.

Recent Poems

Recent Poems (1978) contains only four poems and was published by the small Anvil Press in a limited edition of 400 copies. "From My Diary" is another memory poem. The poet recalls his father speaking of an elderly woman as having been "a great beauty, forty years ago."[17] Now the poet is older than his father was at the time of the remark and "parties sometimes change to funerals." A striking image tolls the passing of the lovers of his decades: "Faces we've once loved / Fit into their seven ages as Russian dolls / Into one another" (*RP,* 4). He can will his memory back to the young face, "shining through all," of the older woman he now loves.

"Late Stravinsky Listening to Late Beethoven" is dedicated to the poet Sacheverell Sitwell and was written after Spender had visited Sitwell's deathbed. It is a particularly fine and moving piece in which language struggles to express the inexpressible, the epiphany of great music played by a great musician. Sitwell "at the end . . . listened only to / Beethoven's Posthumous Quartets" (*RP,* 5). The persona at the bedside sees his friend "weightless as a feather, ecstasy / Shining through pain" as death approaches. He has been "purged of every sense but the transparent / Intelligence." Finally, Sitwell will come to be "one with the thing perceived," the existential end. He will become "Beethoven / Released from deafness into vision, / Stravinsky in that music from his dying" (*RP,* 6). Despair is manageable with the perspective of wisdom, age, and a belief in the unity of life.

"Winter in May" recalls a blizzard in Cincinnati in May 1953 in which the beauty of the snow is quickly trampled underfoot. The poem is another Japanese-style word painting. "A Girl Who Has Drowned Herself Speaks" is a morose poem in which the persona wishes that her drowned body had not been dragged from the river. Left to rot, her "skull would stay—/ But change to crystal" and fish "would swim into / Eye-sockets that looked at them. Thus, "phosphorescent fish," the reality, would live where before "there had been / Ideas of them only, in the brain" (*RP,* 8). The poem pleads to let bodies be, to let flesh return to a comprehending nature where all is one.

Collected Poems, 1928–1985

In making a new collection of his poems in 1986, Spender reorganized his canon into 14 categories, ignoring chronology to some extent and omitting many poems previously included, like "The Funeral." The categories are "I Preludes," his early 1930s poems; "II Exiles"; "III Spain"; "IV A Separation"; "V Elegy for Margaret"; "VI Ambition"; "VII Spiritual Explorations"; "VIII War Poems"; "IX Home"; "X Landscape and Seascape"; "XI Diary Poems"; "XII Word"; "XIII Remembering"; and "XIV Choruses from the Oedipus Trilogy," his translation-adaption of Sophocles.

In *Collected Poems, 1928–1985* (1986) Spender indulged in some unfortunate revisions, "for clarity has always been my aim,"[18] but instead of clarifying he obfuscated, changing some homosexual love poems to make them seem less overt and toning down other early poems to make them seem less radical. The result is generally poetic loss. Readers should go to *Collected Poems, 1928–1953* or to original volumes for the best readings of earlier poems. *Collected Poems, 1928–1985* provides handy and untampered access to Spender's poetry from *Selected Poems* (1964) on.

It is the half dozen new poems written since *The Generous Days* that make *Collected Poems, 1928–1985* important to readers of Spender's poetry, and it is "Auden's Funeral" that is the most moving and significant. The governess-like mentor and friend died on 28 September 1973 in Vienna and was buried in the village of Kirchstetten, where he had lived his last years. Spender attended the funeral.[19] He produced a eulogy evoking Auden's "At the Grave of Henry James." The setting is simple and the language direct. "Auden's Funeral" is a public poem, as the funeral was a public event, but the poem is warm and personal too. In the first section, Spender envisions Auden's face in the coffin as he "cast a clod of earth . . . / Down on the great brass-handled coffin lid. / It rattled on the oak like a door knocker" (*CP* 1986, 184). Spender cannot call his friend back, but Auden, "connivingly sly," is still with him.

The second, third, and fourth sections of "Auden's Funeral" recall student days at Oxford and youthful days in Germany and elsewhere.

Like a ghost, Auden's image keeps coming into view. It is "a Buster Keaton" face. Spender is unable to leave Auden. The fifth section is a farewell, as "your funeral dwindles to its photograph" (*CP* 1986, 188). The impression left is that Spender still loved and greatly missed his lifelong friend, now "happy to be alone, his last work done" (*CP* 1986, 184). "Auden's Funeral" will remain an historic poem.

An earlier poem about Auden, "Auden in Milwaukee," is almost more of an elliptic diary entry than a poem: Auden and Spender are at a student gallery, where Auden is enjoying adulation, but he is really seen "as an object, artifact" (*CP* 1986, 179). Spender realizes this and implies that he, too, an ageing poet, has also become one.

Two other poems also memorialize deceased friends. "Louis Mac-Neice," who died in 1963, "looks down from high heaven / The mocking eyes search-lighting / My ignorance again" (*CP* 1986, 178). Besides graciously praising MacNeice's intelligence, Spender reminds the cognoscenti that he and MacNeice saw many a searchlight when they both served as fire fighters in the Blitz.

"Cyril Connolly," in memory of Spender's coeditor of *Horizon,* is, like "Auden's Funeral," a superior piece, a taut eulogistic sketch only 10 lines long. Spender employs his statuary imagery once more. Death and the poem "make you your statue" and, alas for Connolly, the great conversationalist and gourmet, "deep in the mouth's crevasse / The silent tongue savours / Only the must of dying." Spender has chisled unflattering truth: "Finally, the head is Roman" (*CP* 1986, 181).

"Driving through Snow," written in Connecticut in 1971, finds the poet again encountering "twin circumferences," but this time they are merely on the windshield where the wipers have cleaned. It is a dangerous trip, and the poet is afraid of dying, for there is "the work that must not end before begun" (*CP* 1986, 157). "Grandparents" is forgivable. Spender's son Matthew asks a nun in the hospital, "Is our baby a genius?" (*CP* 1986, 158). The grandparents then go off to the Uffizi and find the paintings of other babies ugly.

Spender the romantic poet has remained true to himself. From the beginning he refused to be a parrot for communist cant or a purveyor of poetic fashions. No one, not Yeats, Eliot, Graves, Thomas, or even the formidable Auden, has pulled Spender the poet from his own orbit around the still center of his small but bright star. In the last thirty years the flow of his poetry has diminished from torrent to trickle because the poet has been distracted by his need to earn a living in letters, diverted by his strong interest in criticism, and by his personal commitment to a more just society, and perhaps, too, as a result of the dislike for his work by F. R. Leavis and the *Scrutiny* establishment,[20] which may have discouraged Spender.

Also, as noted by A. K. Weatherhead, Spender's later poems "are detached from the everyday things of the world and cannot be approached in the workaday frame of mind in which one comes in from the street to read the headlines and throw away the bulk mail."[21] The poet has been truer to his aesthetic than to the requirements and demands of the phenomenal world in which all art must seek to thrive. Yet he has left a luminous record of an era. And like his century in the West, Spender's poetry evolved from the idiom of social struggle, laced with his individual lyric impulse, to implosion and personal expression. Ideology failed and individuality thrived. If, in his early years, the poet was disappointed when he found that his exuberance could not remake the world, his hurt was assuaged when, in his later years, he came to know that he did not have to.

Chapter Four

Injustice with Justice: Fiction and Drama

Stephen Spender has written two novels, two collections of shorter fiction, and a verse play that was produced and acclaimed. He has also translated or cotranslated several dramas by German and classical Greek playwrights. Although poetry is obviously his great creative contribution, his prose fiction and his one original play, *Trial of a Judge,* are intrinsically worth reading and studying. Additionally, they offer historical and biographical insights.

Novels

Spender's two novels are a product of his early years as a writer, but paradoxically they span a lifetime. *The Backward Son* (1940) was published at the end of Spender's miracle decade of poetry, drama, criticism, fiction: the 1930s. *The Temple* (1988) is a revision of a novel Spender began in 1929 and then left in manuscript.

The Backward Son An autobiographical novel centering on events in Spender's childhood, *The Backward Son* is, on another level, a critical history of the rearing and education of the male children of his generation and class. It is a part of the considerable volume of school novels the 1930s produced. The protagonist, Geoffrey Brand, is sent to Tisselthorp House, a private preparatory school, by his preachy father, a Liberal MP and onetime giant figure of a man who collapses into a sorry mess after the untimely death of his wife. The man has been, almost literally, a mountain. On Hampstead Heath he and Geoffrey play at mountain climbing.[1] His head is a "craggy mountain top." As a politician he has achieved the "unscalable heights" of ambition in the grown-up world. His fall from filial grace leaves his son sexually confused.

Geoffrey's fluttering, foolish mother is as great a problem for him. Sent unwillingly to board at Tisselthorp, he hates the school from the first, for he is at once tormented as "Mammy's little Geoff" because his mother was too tenderly demonstrative in front of his schoolmates at the railway platform. Her ultimate "crime" against him, beyond that of sending him away, is her desertion of him by dying after an operation. In Geoffrey's mind, she has abandoned him. There is a final horror for him in their relationship. In his imagination "he saw the stomach with the navel, and just below it a wound cut like a mouth, a wound which they had not sewn-up because it was too late. In thick drops, blood surrounded by water oozed from the wound" (*BS*, 256). Could the 12-year-old Stephen Spender actually have seen this? No wonder the novel ends indecisively and the protagonist is left shocked, depressed, and confused.

The picture of boarding school life is wholly negative. The boys play soccer, collect stamps, and study railway engines, but they are obscene, cruel, snobbish, and bullying. Further, the administration of Tisselthorpe is decidedly Dickensian: the boys are badly fed and badly taught, and the headmaster, Mr. Leather, is a pompous, unctuous, unimaginative, somewhat sadistic pedagogue.

The sensitive Geoffrey loathes everything the headmaster stands for. He can only cry himself to sleep every night after the days loneliness and misery. He meditates on being and nothingness as an existential philosopher might:

Being I means not being Palmer or Daddy or Mummy or Hilary or Christopher. But they also are "I" to themselves. However unhappy they may be, they all say "I am glad that I am I." It would be terrifying to be another. Being I is home.

I shall never know what it is to be them. They must all have their excuses, all be afraid, as I am.

(*BS*, 121)

Although home is also not a happy place for Geoffrey, at least at Christmas he is safe from the terrors of the school. "He is hung at the tiny point of the whole universe, which is his centre of happiness" (*BS*, 113)—a typical Spender image. John Lehmann particularly admired Spender's evocation of a childhood Christmas, calling it "perhaps the most perfectly realized scene in all his prose."[2]

Christmas, however, as the saying goes, comes only once a year, and for poor Geoffrey at school, pathetically, only a machine can succor him in his unhappiness as he tries to get to sleep in his bed. His father had given him a big Ingersoll watch. He tucks it under his ear and listens as

it ticks loudly and lovingly. Its comfort does not come from the fact
that it was a love gift from father, but from the thought of the fidelity
of jewels and springs and spinning wheels in shining metal. "Love
spread from the watch now warmed by his hands and moistened by his
sweat and tears, through the orifice of his ear to his heart, equally
faithful and ticking. The watch loved him. He fell asleep" (*BS,* 100).

The Backward Son is an allegory of man's inhumanity to man and to
child. In true Hobbesian fashion, everyone wants power over fellow
humans and everyone fiercely desires to keep out of the clutch and
control of others. Geoffrey never dares to challenge the tyranny of the
stronger Palmer and Richards, the leading seniors, and he plays syco-
phant even to the disgusting and unpopular Fallow and Like, yet when
his younger brother, Christopher, comes up to school, Geoffrey tyran-
nizes him. What is the point of emancipating the underclass if, given
half a chance, they would immediately oppress others in turn? School is
a microcosm of the totalitarian societies of Stalin and Hitler. With
brutality it prepares boys to endure in an inimical world.

The Backward Son is a confessional novel that Spender used to rid
himself of a lot of pain and hostility: his love-hate relationship with his
father and other authority figures, his Oedipal frustrations, his feelings
of childhood abandonment at being left unhappily at boarding school,
and his repressed resentment of the domination of strong women in his
childhood and youth, notably his mother and his Aunt Schuster. However, the novel is marred in that it sometimes reads as inappropriate
parody and in that, lacking objectivity, it "doth protest too much."

The Temple   First penned in 1929, but left in manuscript form
because Faber considered it libelous and pornographic, *The Temple* was
unearthed by Spender and rewritten.[3] It is an autobiographical novel in
two parts, the first set in the Weimar Germany of 1929; the second part
was also originally set in 1929 but was now changed to 1932 in order,
as Spender says in his introduction, to heighten the "encroaching atmosphere of dark politics covering the whole landscape . . . into which
my German characters are moving" (*T,* xii).

The Temple is primarily concerned with the youthful male body, as
appreciated by a handsome young Englishman at a time when the sense
of sexual liberation in Germany, so different from the situation in
puritanical Britain, mingled with feverish political excitement: the
deadly struggle between Weimar democracy, international communism, and rising fascism.

The temple is the place of pagan worship as well as the human body in which we all live and of which the protagonist, Paul, an Oxford student on vacation in Germany, is especially admiring. He enjoys seeing photos of beautiful naked men:

One, in particular, struck Paul. It was of a bather standing naked at the reed-fringed edge of a lake. The picture was taken slightly from below so that the torso, rising above the thighs, receded, and the whole body was seen, layer on layer of hips and rib-cage and shoulders, up to the towering head, with dark hair helmeted against a dark sky. V-shaped shadows of willow leaves fell like showers of arrows on San Sebastian, on the youth's sunlit breast and thighs. "Oh, wonderful!" said Paul, "The temple of the body!"

(*T*, 69)

The San Sebastian image is a well-known homoerotic icon.

Paul has left his Oxford classes and his friends Marston and Wilmot, and come to Germany at the invitation of a wealthy German friend he made at college, Ernst Stockmann, whose Jewish background begins to cause him trouble in Part Two, although he and his parents remain quite sure that important capitalists like themselves will be safe in the totalitarian Germany evolving. Ernst falls in love with Paul and pursues him avidly, until finally Paul, out of kindness more than physical attraction, has sex with him. It is Paul's first sexual experience, and the next day, on the beach, he has his second, with the girl Irmie. "Germany's the Only Place for Sex. England's No Good" (*T*, 7) is the succinct sexual theme of this very contemporary and readable novel, which is a struggle against the all-pervasive censorship of pre—World War II Britain. A friend of Paul's cries out, "I want to leave this country where censors ban James Joyce and the police raid the gallery where D. H. Lawrence's pictures are on show" (*T*, 16).

Structurally, *The Temple* consists of a series of holiday trips and tours to resorts and beaches where young men of homosexual inclination sport and gambol. The book's weakness is that the serious political dimensions are nearly lost in the self-absorption of Paul and his privileged friends. Sexual politics obscure public politics. When Paul, who is professedly radical, finally does connect with a working-class boy, in Part Two, it is to patronize him and take a nude photo of him. The pagan youths of Weimar only have eyes for themselves. They are mostly doomed to a destruction emblematized by the pink triangle.

The Temple is a verisimilitudinous document of a special time and place. It will be continued to be read for what it records, the interwar Germany more famously recounted it Christopher Isherwood's *Berlin Stories*. Indeed, there are characters in *The Temple* fairly obviously modeled on Isherwood and Auden. At its best, Spender's novel offers passages of sheer lyrical beauty, as when Paul watches his friend Heinrich balance himself on a narrow edge of rock: "Paul watched the surface of rippling muscle which sprang upwards from the thighs, across the body, to the roots of his arms. The direction, the impulse of his body was simple yet complex—a single gesture of a statue's eloquent extended hand" (*I*, 123).

The Temple was clearly unpublishable in the 1930s. Spender must have realized that. It is therefore probable that he wrote the novel primarily for himself and his friends, although there was the possibility of publication in France. Writing *The Temple* in 1929 was an act of rebellion and defiance; revising and publishing it in 1988 was an act of truth and nostalgia.

Short Fiction

Stephen Spender has published two collections of stories. *The Burning Cactus* (1936) is a youthful work depicting his desire to find a unity of spirit and body in fiction as well as poetry. *Engaged in Writing, and The Food and the Princess* (1958) are mature satires on what was happening in postwar Europe to the once-incandescent dream of a better world.

Spender's shorter fiction is sometimes heavy-handed and overwritten, dialogue is not his forte, and characterization sometimes does not stand up well in regard to plausibility. However, Spender's plots are skillfully crafted around a single protagonist and appropriately limited incidents, all serving to establish and enhance the general theme of the individual's right to a freedom of action that allows him or her to succeed or fail, to prosper or decline, to act wisely or foolishly—in other words, to be human.

The Burning Cactus   The five stories in *The Burning Cactus* are very early Spender, displaying his values and the subjects of interest to him before the age of 25. They were written between 1927 and 1935, but mostly from 1933 to 1935. The collection is dedicated to W. H. Auden and T. A. R. Hyndman. The stories are poetic, graceful, and cinematic, especially the novella "The Dead Island," a study in neurotic character in which a rich, emancipated, sensuous woman separated from her third husband is sexually aroused by a young manic depressive male dancer she meets at a resort. She has been sexually frustrated in her marriages by men who did not meet her needs, and therefore, "spiritually, she has never ceased to be a virgin."[4] The situation is right out of D. H. Lawrence.

Here the young man's neurotic, sexually ambivalent, self-destructive character is symbolic of Europe's social morbidity. He, like it, is beyond help. He longs to escape to the Dead Island offshore, his Elysium. Nevertheless, when called upon, he is good in bed. His lovemaking seems to her like the music of Mozart, and he brings her to orgasm: "The man now eclipsed her, covering her head with unquenchable blackness, and with a spading body forcing her to enter the circle of the temple and the dance" (*BC,* 24). The relationship is tortured and unstable, and they separate. He returns to psychiatric care and his male lover. For the last time, she climbs a hill, where she "dismissed her own problems and thought instead of the appalling loneliness of the young man who had set out to the Dead Island, to Egypt, to his death" (*BC,* 94). In feeling love and seeing disintegration, the protagonist has come to understand something of the ecstatic and despairing range of human nature, that all live on the edge, and that each is a solitary traveler. "The dead are heaped together. But the living are alone" (*BC,* 96).

"The Dead Island" is an intriguing story, as disturbing and erotic as anything Spender has written and much more psychologically insightful than most of the fiction of its time. The atmosphere of decadence and decay is comparable to that in Thomas Mann's *Death in Venice* (1913). The story's ultimate subject is the element Spender believed he was living in: the destructive element.

"The Cousins" is another Spender self-portrait, this time as a German alter ego. Werner, a German-Jewish cousin of the sons of the English Lord Edward, is "bony with light hair, a dreamy look overlaid with traces of anxiety in a certain fussiness of the brow, veiling the clear eyes and high forehead as a wire netting overlays a green lawn; he had altogether a too sensitive expression" (*BC,* 104). Werner, a socialist, does not find money vulgar but only a means "of escaping vulgarity. His Socialism immediately called for income of at least one thousand pounds a year" (*BC,* 108). Werner is a pacifist and an aesthete. In the end, he cuts short his visit to his English relatives because they are too selfish, too insensitive, too healthy, too normal, too superficial, too careless with the world, too self-deluding, and too uninvolved with life. Spender has stepped out of his caste to rake it.

The title story, one of the more successful stories in the collection, contains yet another Spender self-portrait in Till, a sexually confused and ambivalent young man. The protagonist's "open collar revealed a graceful eager neck: he had a fair but not unblemished complexion, long fair hair, good features, large eyes and sensitive nostrils" (*BC*, 154). Till's life is like dry, bitter, cutting cactus. In his destructive element he sets fire to a hillside, menacing a community. His friends, male and female, betray him. In the end, he feels that, like a burning cactus, he has been consumed in the flame of a living hell.

In reviewing *The Burning Cactus*, Graham Greene, noted that the collection as a whole indicated that "the umbilical cord had not been cut," implying amateurishness and perhaps incompletion, "except for the fine title story." Green saw skill in the story's imagery and mood setting, "but it is in the figure of the suffering posing hysterical homosexual of the title story that a profound social awareness of things as they are combines with a poet's personal fantasy to create a work of art."[5]

"Two Deaths" is more realistic than the other stories in *The Burning Cactus*. Set in the politically turbulent Vienna of 1934, it is about the death of an old Austrian socialist mortally wounded in the street fighting. His death is contrasted with the assassination of the dictator Dollfuss, as if destiny had decided to equate the two in the name of justice. The story is related in the first person. The persona, a young Englishman, has taken his friend Tony to a hospital to have his appendix removed. The hospital symbolizes the sick Austrian society. There free Austria is dying. "Two Deaths" recreates the atmosphere of those turbulent days as clearly as Spender portrays them in *World within World* and almost as sensitively as he deals with them in *Vienna*.

"By the Lake" was first written in 1927 and later rewritten. Spender had intended it to be the beginning of a novel (*BC*, 265). The protagonist, an English student named Richard Birney, is staying in a pension in Lausanne in order to perfect his French. There he meets Donald, an English boy who is a scion of the nobility. A fast friendship develops between them, even though Richard cannot afford to keep up with his wealthy friend. They make a boat trip to the Byron-sung castle at Chillon. Spender takes the opportunity to get in a fashionable swipe at Americans: "The guardrooms, halls, dungeons, and passages were full of Americans reading aloud from Baedekers, peering behind tapestries, endeavouring to pry open chests, carving their names on pillars, or frankly rushing round" (*BC,* 227).

Richard is an atheist and Donald is a devout Christian. Richard is also sexually attracted to Donald as their friendship deepens. They compare school experiences and find them sadly similar. Spender has Richard explain how the boarding school inadvertently encourages homosexuality:

Well think, what happens at school, how miserable you are, because you are always wanting to know about sex. How you continually think yourself wicked and believe that no one else can be as wicked as you are. Yet all the time, really, everyone around is occupied with the same thoughts and concealing them. The masters keep you as busy as possible with work and games, and stamp-collecting and debating, so that you have no time to think about this dreadful thing and no time to think either about the other more beautiful things that make life worth living. Then, when you're about sixteen, at an age when the milkboy and the grocer's and errand boys are walking out with their first girls, you fall in love with some cherubic looking boy in a lower form, who has a clear skin and blue eyes and who needs protecting.

(*BC,* 240)

Richard thinks he has seduced Donald, and he makes his way into his friend's bed, but Donald is only trying to convert him, to save him, and "Richard got out of bed and went back to his room" (*BC,* 264). Spender is bold with this story. The boys really do not know what to do about sexuality. They are caught between innocence and knowledge, and in a surprising way for Spender, their innocence is saved, at least for the time being, by the faith of one of them.

The stories in *The Burning Cactus* are treatises on escape: from England; from the rigidity, hypocrisy, and puritanism of school; from parental control; from childhood fears; from sexual stereotyping; and, most of all, from societal oppression. As D. E. S. Maxwell points out, "In all these stories, social organisation has built up a 'cage of institutions,' of which marriage and family are as much a part as its bigger, more impersonal mechanisms. Together, they compose 'a machinery of anxiety' whose operation affects all individuals while remaining beyond their control."[6]

Engaged in Writing, and The Fool and the Princess   Of the two novellas in the collection, the first is by far the stronger work, although it is marred by prose as heavy as lead. *Engaged in Writing* is a statement of disillusionment, a bitter satire on the vanity and mendacity of European intellectuals. It is also an exposé of the pomposity, the arrogance, the posturing, and the futility of many internationally recognized authors. They are depicted as word machines dehumanized by their egos as much as by their occupation. Unsettled by his post–World War II stint with UNESCO and a 1956 meeting of the European Cultural Association in Venice, Spender meant to draw blood from those intellectuals who, in his view, misused the public trust, either because of ideological extremism or venality.

In *Engaged in Writing,* a 50-year-old British ex-Communist and novelist, Olin Asphalt, is to represent the United Nations cultural agency LITUNO at a weeklong East–West conference of European intellectuals in Venice, organized by Dr. Bonvolio, head of EUROPLUME. It is March 1956, just after the Khrushchev speech to the Twentieth Communist Party Congress, attacking Stalinism. The purpose of the Venice conference is to find out where "engagement" now stands. It doesn't stand anywhere. The old cold war intellectual guerrillas cannot change their ingrained ways. Disillusioned, Asphalt comes to realize that the main issue of the conference is what to discuss at the next conference. Bureaucracies are self-perpetuating. Self-preservation is their secret agenda and true goal. Angered and nearly febrile over this revelation, Asphalt disowns his fellow intellectuals and resigns from LITUNO. It is better to be engaged in writing than in useless mind games with "experts," who in fact are not interested in real, human issues. The world is shut out of "the hermetically canned talk of the intellectuals."[7]

A chief weakness of the novella is the cardboard character of the protagonist. Again Spender is not good with dialogue. Furthermore, it is difficult to find anyone to care about in the story. As a social satire, the novella achieves a degree of success; as fiction, it fails.

The Fool and the Princess, started in 1946, put aside, and then finished in 1957, is less of an achievement than *Engaged in Writing.* This story of Harry Granville, a British displaced-persons official—the "fool" of the title—who falls in love with an ersatz refugee princess in a former concentration camp and nearly leaves his wife and child for her, is simply not credible. The refugee is saintly, the wife forgiving, the best friend dastardly, and the protagonist tepid. His adventure in infidelity results in a single kiss in a cab but leaves him well satisfied. His attempt to set up a "captain's paradise" in England and Germany is as logical as Brownian movement. Still, the dialogue in *The Fool and the*

Princess is more fluid and skillful than in *Engaged in Writing*. As in the first novella, Spender here seems to be trying to get something off his chest.

Of the two collections, *The Burning Cactus* is the superior by far. Those stories are close to Spender's best poetry in subject, theme, language, and execution. They emerged from the same creative fire that produced *Twenty Poems* and *The Still Centre*—the passion of a committed, involved, major poet in his twenties.

Drama

Trial of a Judge   Written for London's left-leaning Group Theatre and performed at the United Theatre in Camden Town in 1937, *Trial of a Judge* (1939) is a five-act Elizabethan-style verse drama.[8] In an essay entitled "Poetry and Expressionism," Spender argues that all poetry is dramatic, and all serious drama, in verse or prose, is poetic in that both forms transcend realism to reach a core of universal significance. Poetic drama can thus be an effective medium for social awareness and change because it can force "the complacent middle-class theatre-going public [to look] outwards from themselves and their families to a picture of an extensive conflict which had the world as its scene, and in which their lives are less significant than pawns."[9] This is a position that Eliot had taken earlier. In *Trial of a Judge,* Spender was clearly trying to do for politics what Eliot had done for religion in *Murder in the Cathedral* (1935): to place it above temporality and selfish mundanity.

In his play, Spender tests his ideology. Caught between the violent forces of the time, communism and fascism, Spender identifies with his judge, who, despite his naive liberal precepts, emerges as the only noble human being in the play, precisely because he is an open-minded liberal. His democratic idealism is his glory.

In a mythic country where fascists are coming to power; the judge is faced with the task of condemning three young fascist murderers who have brutally killed a Communist, supposedly a Jew. For them, murder was "their racial privilege."[10] They trumpet their racism:

> Let the biped stand, let the nordic
> Sunhaired head be matched against cloud drifts
> And the whip hand crack the lightning
> Canine and eye teeth laugh in the sun's face.

His flags never dip except for night
Or their momentary mutual salute
Or to utter surrender—yet Western Man
Less proud than happy standards of bunting
Is barked by dogs, governed by servants,
Gutted by the Jew, reproached by niggers.
Return, O gentlemen of the field, to your primary
hunting!

(TJ, 14)

Pressure is brought to free the prisoners. An old classmate of the judge, now an unprincipled politician, tries to get him to revoke his judgment in the case and instead only condemn three Communists who carried guns and clashed with police. The judge's wife supports the friend. Reluctantly the judge yields, recognizing that it is a tragic sacrifice of principle and conscience: "We are trampled beneath a brutal present / Far realer than our life-long dream" *(TJ,* 39). But compromise with conscience only leads to a fascist cell for the judge. He is tried for high treason, ironically, by his former friend, and he pleads guilty, "for by your law, the jungle / Is established; and the tiger's safety is guaranteed / When he hunts his innocent victim" *(TJ,* 75). The friend is stricken with remorse and retracts the condemnation, but he is seized and imprisoned. His attempt to save the judge is to no avail. The fascist subversion and victory is complete when the judge is executed by a firing squad.

In *Trial of a Judge,* justice is shown to be the major casualty when a state lurches violently to the right. By implication, a radical swerve left produces the same result. The tortured and complex imagery of the verse play, difficult but not impossible to grasp in the theater, as both Shakespeare and Yeats remind us, brilliantly parallels the mental and physical suffering of the humanist judge and those people in the middle who support him. Even today, in light of the world's sad experience in the last 50 years, *Trial of a Judge* is shocking and effective, an underrated and neglected drama of great symbolic power. It works as both theater and poetry.

Chapter Five
Destructive and Creative: Literary Criticism

Stephen Spender's career as a literary critic has been almost as long and nearly as distinguished as his career as a poet. It has given him sufficient academic cachet to gain him entrance to many universities in Britain and the United States as a lecturer and visiting professor, culminating in his prestigious appointment as professor of English at the University of London. Furthermore, literary criticism has been a most important intellectual exercise for Spender the romantic, forcing him to look carefully at the work of other writers and adopt aesthetic and historical perspectives that later influenced his own work. Translation has served a similar function for Spender. In the long run, Spender's literary criticism, excellent as it is, will primarily be only of historical interest, while the poetry will remain a part of the canon of twentieth-century British literature. Spender's work as a critic will always be a useful servant to those scholars wishing to comprehend not only the significance of his poetry but also the chief literary values and perceptions of his time.

In more than 40 years of work as a literary critic, from "Poetry and Revolution" (1933) through *The Thirties and After* (1979), Spender's critical position has remained constant: he is a personalist and a positivist. His perspective is empirical, totally nonmetaphysical, programmatic, and immediate. Spender stands amid the critical fray, creating, recording, and cutting, all at the same time. He would surely insist that although reality is dangerous to intellectuals and idealists, it nevertheless remains the standard against which one measures relevance in art.

Stephen Spender's first work of literary criticism is the essay "Poetry and Revolution," first published in *New Country.* Having come under the influence of Marxist thinking, he needed to tranpose his own bourgeois experience as a writer, out of which he would normally write for a well-educated, privileged class, into an art that could serve all of society. It was not enough to be a romantic rebel ranting in isolation and promoting an incoherent philosophy of discontent with capitalism. The need was to rework bourgeois art into a tool for the overthrow of a corrupt society and for the construction of a virtuous one. In other words, by becoming a "practical revolutionary," by adopting the objectives and social symbols of Marxism, the bourgeois writer, perhaps sacrificing some of his individualism, can help bring about the new society.

In "Poetry and Revolution," says Samuel Hynes, "the great problem that Spender deals with is one that every artist in the thirties had to face: what is the right relation between art and action?"[1] Ultimately, however, Spender's position in "Poetry and Revolution" is a defense against the new mode of discourse advanced by dogmatic communist theorists, wherein art is to be judged solely for its programmability and propaganda value. For Spender, the artist can never abandon his or her culture. Spender realizes that he simply has not inherited a proletarian tradition. He can only serve the revolution by telling revolutionaries the truth. The artist stands above the political fray and, like Shelley, exercises authority through his or her higher moral position.

Poetry is less suited for propaganda than prose because it conveys truth emotionally, through the individual reader's sensibility-led response to a word-crafted situation. It cannot directly advocate action and remain poetry. Poetry is language preserved in the plasma of truth: "It records the changing of words and fixes their meanings, it preserves certain words in their pure and historic meaning, it saves language from degeneration into looseness" (*NC*, 69). Clearly, poetry is too holy to suffer the profanation of propaganda.

The Destructive Element

Spender took the title for his most important work of literary criticism from a phrase in Joseph Conrad's *Lord Jim,* as alluded to in I. A. Richards's *Science and Poetry* (1926): "In the destructive element, immerse."[2] Essentially, the point of the title is to alert one that human nature and values are precarious, not immutable, and that the forces of destruction facing them are enormous. The temptation is for immolation and a *Götterdämmerung* death. It must be resisted. This resistance is at the heart of Spender's lifelong philosophy. He saw the writers of the initial third of the century as if they were amazed savages witnessing their first fire and wondering whether or not to embrace that new destructive element. They did not. He must not.

The embodiments of the destructive element for Spender in 1935 were World War I, the Great Depression, and the rise of fascism. "Political chaos" was fostered by weak liberalism and strong capitalism, an axiom also advanced in *Forward from Liberalism* (1937). The greats of the century whom he chooses to discuss in *The Destructive Element* (1935)—Henry James, T. S. Eliot, William Butler Yeats, and D. H. Lawrence—were all "faced by the destructive element, that is by the experience of an all-pervading Present, which is a world without belief."[3] The thrust of *The Destructive Element* is that great literature must be reread in terms of the present, and the present's signature is social revolution. Reality is destructive, but the artist must not reject it, even though he or she may be frightened and appalled by it. The artist must immerse "self" in it, avoid destruction, and not retreat to a mythic past or revert to an idiosyncratic distortion.

Spender's chapters on James are especially perceptive. Although James "revolutionized the method of presentation in the novel, altering the emphasis from the scene to that intellectual and imaginative activity which leads to the scene, so that his scenes are symptoms, not causes" (*DE,* 16), Spender takes him to task for believing "that the only values which mattered at all were those cultivated by individuals who had escaped from the general decadence of Europe" (*DE,* 17). James thus withdrew his art "from the objective world, until he had created a world of his own, in which it was possible for that reality to appear either in a form in which it was beautifully accepted . . . or in which it was 'shown up' in its fullest horror" (*DE,* 36).

For Spender, Eliot's *The Waste Land* is the best description of a world without belief. But, paradoxically, Eliot had sought refuge from that world in myths from Sir James Frazer's *The Golden Bough,* an imagined church tradition, and "firm belief . . . in the possibility of personal salvation" (*DE,* 135). He thus became "blinded to the existence of people outside himself" (*DE,* 146). Therefore, Eliot, whose characters are not "alive," is himself on the side of death. The legacy of his despair must be overcome if younger writers are to serve society.

Yeats retreated to a magical system not very different from Eliot's retreat to myth and orthodoxy. Yeats's reader is "at every stage perplexed. . . . He imagines that all is to be mystery and twilight and that he dare hardly listen, he must be so silent, for fear lest he disturb the fairies" (*DE,* 127). But Yeats is truly distinguished when he works in the sphere of realism. His great weakness is that he "has found as yet, no subject of moral significance in the social life of his time" (*DE,* 131).

For D. H. Lawrence, "sex . . . is life, it is the very opposite of death . . . and it is the means of escape for the individual from the living death of the modern world" (*DE,* 178). Lawrence's greatness lies in his siding as an artist with the whole of civilization. He was not merely a supporter of a clique. Lawrence recognized that external nature has a vivid life of its own, independent of human life. Most important, he was deeply interested in the political and moral questions of his day. Thus, he was a "revolutionary and a preacher." His values were living and real. Life for him was real, sex was real, death was real. The essential—that is, not existential—ideas of love and honor could always be sacrificed to reality. Spender also discusses Joyce, Kafka, and Wilfred Owen in *The Destructive Element.* They are important but lesser modernists to him.

The Destructive Element remains an eminently readable and useful work of literary criticism. It is a committed but not obdurate leftist view of the values and functions of twentieth-century literature. The perspective is that of a critic attempting to shed the constricting skin of a bourgeois. Although *The Destructive Element* has been interpreted as a call for a degree of restriction on artistic freedom in the name of service to society, it is more accurately described as an appeal to artists to open their eyes to the social and political whirlwind in which they live and to accept the truth of the existence of their personal heart of darkness. Thus, the subject of art must be moral, and it is the individual artist who decides what is moral, a position unacceptable to fervent communist theorists.

The New Realism

Spender's 24-page monograph *The New Realism* is a defense of poetry. Spender insists that realism involves, not an imitation, but a deep analysis of the society in which he and his contemporaries are living. That kind of in-depth analysis is bound to be revolutionary. Modern literature should be evaluated in terms of how much of life is portrayed honestly and truthfully.

Spender argues that "the duty of the artist is to remain true to the standards which he discovers only within himself."[4] His job is to analyze, not to change. In rejecting activism and insisting that bourgeois writers can only analyze their world, Spender breaks completely with the extreme left-wing political commitment of many writers of his generation. "Writers who have attempted to throw off their bourgeois environment to enter a revolutionary one, have only succeeded in uprooting themselves, in getting killed, or in ceasing to be writers and becoming politicians" (*NR*, 19). Samuel Hynes says that this "passage reads like a farewell to the hopes and illusions of the mid-decade, the years when action seemed possible."[5]

Life and the Poet

Spender continues to distance himself from Marxist critical values in *Life and the Poet* (1942): "A society with no values outside politics is a machine carrying its human cargo, with no purposes in its institutions reflecting their cares, eternal aspirations, loneliness, need for love."[6] He is concerned over the compromise and the corruption of the intellectual in wartime. Regardless of the stress of the moment and the rectitude of the cause, the intellectual must not give up his "writing, his research, his studio, to appear on a public platform. After a time his credit as a writer, scientist or artist is exhausted" (*LP*, 9).

Spender views society not as "a machine of mutually destructive means, but an organic growth around a central philosophy of life and a wide understanding of the needs of satisfactory living" (*LP*, 23). Spender seems somewhat indebted for the concept to Alfred North Whitehead, who sees life on all levels building its own environment through creative "societies of cooperating organisms."[7] For Whitehead, the environment has a degree of plasticity influenced by creativity and morality, and for Spender, artists create in their fellow humans "a realisation of their own nature, a love for their fellow-beings, an attitude of mind in which they are willing to accept change for the sake of a fuller life, and having accepted it, to incorporate their sense of life in political institutions" (*LP*, 25). Cooperation is the essence of positive political change, and the artist is the moral arbiter of that change.

Although Spender feels that espousal of religion is often an act of self-deception, he is willing to allow for a "religious attitude" within his definition of humanism. There is much truth in the Christian view of life. Indeed, "there is room for some unknown quantity which we might call God. But because scepticism admits the unknown, that does not mean that it releases the floodgates to all the minds which claim that the unknown is precisely what they know. The mysteries are mysteries, the speculation is speculation, the God remains without a name" (*LP*, 59). The breakdown of religion leads to the breakdown of morality and that is the last thing Spender wishes to see happen. Many people cannot lead moral and ethical lives without the structure of

Christianity. Yet "it is possible to find reasons for this wisdom without returning to the authority of the Churches" (LP, 64).

Finally, Spender discusses the role of experience in the development of the artist: "A great artist does not have to travel, fight, be terrified, freeze, boil. He already has sufficient experience of his own mind and body and social environment to be conscious of all these possibilities. It is only a lesser artist who needs to be shaken by events into awareness of what, if he had the patience to realise it, he could discover from his own memory" (LP, 125). Spender was retreating into his own personality and finding the subjects for his poems in the examination of self. It is logical that from this personalist position he would offer introspection as a means of access to greater achievement in art. After all, "poetry is concerned with being, and being is infinite" (LP, 127).

In the darkest hours of World War II, Spender, as depressed as anyone, nevertheless tried to instill hope and direction in the poetry-reading and art-loving public through *Life and the Poet*. To a considerable extent he succeeded. A bridge was built over chaos, and the brilliant past would remain connected to the future society waiting to be born when the guns were silenced.

Poetry since 1939

Published for the British Council, *Poetry since 1939* (1946) is concerned with the question of how six years of total war had affected the state and production of British poetry. The book is directed to the American and continental audiences, which to one degree or another were out of touch with the British literary scene. Spender discusses the adverse conditions under which poets had to work while serving in the armed forces, performing war work, and losing outlets as publishing was severely restricted during the war because of the shortage of paper. Spender lists the war efforts of most of the major British poets. Generously, Spender says of Auden, "His American freedom enabled him to improve his technique enormously, so that he is now the most accomplished technician writing poetry in the English language" (PS39, 10–11).

Spender declares that British wartime poetry is little different in quality from what was written before the war, although critical opinion has contradicted this view, considering wartime poetry as having declined from prewar standards. He was surely correct in calling Eliot's *Four Quartets* the outstanding poetry of the war (PS39, 13–14).

Spender's summation of Eliot in 1946 was shared by almost all British and most American poets and critics: "He may well be the greatest poetic influence in the world today" (*PS39*, 17).

For Spender, Edith Sitwell is a unique poet, with "a rare and aristocratic quality of imagination." Her imagery in her wartime poetry is "jewel-like." (*PS39*, 20). John Masefield's 1942 poem "The Land Workers" is "mature, ripe, golden . . . perhaps the crown of his achievement" (*PS39*, 22), while Robert Graves and Edwin Muir are also singled out for accolades. But Auden, Day Lewis, MacNeice, and Spender, as "the Poets of the Thirties," receive the greatest attention. Spender outlines the group's history. He notes their special sense of community and sagaciously comments that "despite an almost exhibitionist attitude towards sex, these poets rather lacked sensuality, and their approach to all problems was intellectual" (*PS39*, 28). The master is still Auden, "the most brilliant poet of his generation in England" (*PS39*, 29). Of the rest of the Oxford Group, he understates, "There was a tendency for the poetry of Day Lewis, MacNeice, and Spender to turn inwards towards a personal subject matter and to avoid the world of outer events" (*PS39*, 34).

Spender discusses the new poetry of younger, lesser known poets like William Empson, George Barker, and David Gascoyne, but he reserves his greatest praise for Dylan Thomas, who "is perhaps the only one capable of exercizing a literary influence as great as that of Auden" (*PS39*, 45). It might have come about if Thomas had not died so young. Spender is happy with the poetry of the time. It is a worthy representative of a great tradition. It has a perceptive, interested audience. "Modern English poetry is alive" (*PS39*, 63).

Poetry since 1939 is good reading. One gets a sense of being in a particular place and time as older and younger poets are struggling to keep the flame of poetry alive in a dark moment. Spender's judgments, although typically generous, are still sound today.

Shelley

Written for the British Council pamphlet series on writers, *Shelley* (1952) is a workmanlike introduction of the life and works of the romantic poet who had the greatest influence on Spender. During the 1930s and even the early 1940s, Spender was frequently compared to Shelley. The 56-page monograph focuses on the significance of Shelley as an artist and as a cultural revolutionary. Spender's admiration for the great romantic is evident throughout the work, as he develops two themes: the beauty and skill of his poetry and the greatness of his spirit.

The Creative Element

Based on a series of lectures given at the University of Cincinnati, where Spender held the Elliston Chair of Poetry, *The Creative Element* (1953) ranks just after *The Destructive Element.* Here the emphasis is on the processes of art. Spender feels that he had placed too much emphasis on the creative energies of individual writers who confronted that destructiveness but who overvalued the social context of their work as they tried to effect a pattern of society where human rights are respected by all.

Whereas the destructive element consists of the external forces of chaos and the internal forces of corruption, "the creative element is the individual vision of the writer who realizes in his work the decline of modern values while isolating his own individual values from the context of society. He never forgets the modern context, in fact he is always stating it, but he does so only to create the more forcibly the visions of his own isolation."[8]

Yet, in some ways, *The Creative Element* is a more pessimistic document than *The Destructive Element:* "So perhaps the 'destructive element' was not, as I thought, capitalism, fascism, the political mechanism which produced wars and unemployment. It was simply society itself. Genius had renounced, or moved outside, society, and any acceptance of a social concept which threatened individual isolation was destructive to its unique vision" (*CE,* 12).

Thus, Spender confesses again to the political "mistakes" of his youth, feeling now, probably incorrectly, that he had contributed to the denigration of the role of the artist and the importance of art in society. *The Destructive Element* proposes that the way out of the destructive void of modern society is for artists and others to align themselves with a progressive "ism" that could deal effectively with the complex moral, social, and economic problems that were destroying the world. Although great artists like Henry James had created their own worlds, such escapism would not do for artists of the present and the future. In *The Creative Element,* Spender shifts attitudes and argues that artists must look within themselves to generate answers to society's problems. No "ism" is intrinsically superior. Danger lies in fervently embracing any system.

Spender opines that modern society is antithetic to creativity and has devalued it. The poet is being driven out of the world. The edifices and machines about which Spender and Auden had once sung in exaltation are now threatening and dehumanizing. The poet's imagination cannot defeat them: "Modern man in the industrial city is like a mouse who has given birth to a litter of mountains, mountains which are not like natural mountains because they don't stay put. They don't become scenery, the background of the human drama. They are mountains, so to speak, which work on their own steam and function beyond the control of their inventors. They are mountains which may fall on us" (*CE,* 38).

The answer perhaps is that a great poet is needed, one who will transcend the modern artist's need for isolation and political purity, who will not die with a dying society because he or she will give society new life engendered in personal creativity and a forward-looking "new system which will give meaning to the world" (*CE,* 52). Furthermore, politics and politicians need to embrace humanism. Indeed, "politics should be Christian." The process of history is not an inevitable dialectic. Individual rights need not be subordinated to the so-called greater good. "The answer to Marxism is to accept the challenge of the necessity of worldwide social change, but at the same time to regard the individual with Christian charity and justice" (*CE,* 199).

Spender expostulates on the danger to the artist when he places himself at the disposal of sociopolitical orthodoxies. Even in the West, government bodies and private foundations, ostensibly well-meaning, are sometimes ideologically insinuating, consciously or unconsciously exacting conformist views from artists and interfering with the artistic process. In America the universities subject artists to a paternalism that traps the creative spirit. Intellectual censorship can be more subtly pervasive than most people realize.

For Spender, Shelley may be the best example of the great artist as individual and rebel. His social vision was all-encompassing, and although he did not change the world appreciably, he kept his ideals fresh and clear in his mind and passed them on to humankind unsullied. In that the imaginative life of artists provides roots for a society, "poets are the unacknowledged legislators of mankind." Shelley's vision still seems true to "a conceivable future because it is true of man's feeling about his own nature" (*CE,* 28). Great visionaries like Shelley are Spender's heroes. Blake, Keats, Baudelaire, James, Rimbaud, Rilke, and Yeats are in his pantheon. He also admires Woolf, Forster,

Joyce, and Eliot, but he considers them lesser figures. If only contemporary art could recover the genius, dedication, insights, and world-encompassing spirit of the "greats."

The possibilities of poetry remain substantial: "Poetry could not become a substitute for religion, but it could draw or create a picture of the blank of religion and describe the modern human experiences to which the religions no longer seemed to apply. It could . . . show that it is not enough to have sensibility and the imagination. It is necessary imaginatively to systematize the world of the imagination" (*CE,* 177).

In *The Creative Element,* Spender finds faith in humanism alive. This faith is extremely significant for the future of humankind, and without it, poets will not be remembered by history. Without humanism, Spender's life, thought, and times will be forgotten. *The Creative Element* reminds us that the poet creates worlds within the imagination and, through artistry, gives us that world, making our own significant in the process. The creative element is indispensable to our existence.

The Making of a Poem

In his introduction to *The Making of a Poem* (1955), Spender calls the 12 essays included "the notes of a writer on writing."[9] They form a mosaic, serving as a practicum in writing. Spender discusses works and authors that have been of major influence on him and that have affected his creative development. He singles out Shakespeare, Blake, and Keats. He also addresses Georgian poetry, Housman, Auden, Dylan Thomas, American writing, and other subjects.

The title essay, a study in the psychology of composition, is useful for young poets, as it is full of nuts and bolts. Spender says that a poet "should have certain qualifications of ear, vision, imagination, memory, and so on. He should be able to think in images, he should have as great a mastery of language as a painter has over his palette." Spender plays down the significance of inspiration; rather, "a poet has to adapt himself . . . to the demands of his vocation" (*MP,* 45). Spender then goes on to discuss the importance of concentration, and he provides some techniques to obtain that state. As always for him, memory is of great significance: "Poets have this highly developed sensitive apparatus of memory" (*MP,* 55). Spender illustrates his own technique by taking the reader through the writing of a poem. An accomplished poet might find the essay simplistic, but a neophyte would do well to study it carefully. "The Making of a Poem" essay is a sharp tool.

The essay "Greatness of Aim" is an interesting comparison of intention in "two poets as different as Mr. W. H. Auden and Dylan Thomas." They are both poets who began to write before theorizing, yet both "aimed at putting a whole view of life derived from his whole experience into a poetry moulded and developed with that purpose" (*MP*, 35). Both poets became great in their very different ways. Both are strikingly original. It could be said that Auden is Apollonian and Thomas Dionysian, but what is really important is that both grasped as much of modern life as they were "capable of imaginatively digesting" (*MP*, 44).

For Spender, A. E. Housman "is the lyricist of English repression" (*MP*, 158), while Goethe's development, so "deeply influenced by one English poet: Shakespeare; and almost obsessively preoccupied with the legend of one English contemporary poet: Byron" (*MP*, 119), remains an illustration of what is of utmost importance to the character of a great poet. Goethe is "the supreme example to our period since the French Revolution of the struggle with subjectivism, which he overcame . . . by absorbing into himself the subjective, negative, self-pitying tendencies and relating them to objective knowledge and objective living and past tradition, through a deliberate act of will" (*MP*, 134). The will again. The power source of the artist. The true muse and inspiration.

In "American Diction V. American Poetry," Spender faults American poets for trying to make each poem a manifesto, whereas the English poet is more relaxed because "he thinks of himself as existing within a cultural tradition" (*MP*, 172). Spender is not on target in this essay, especially when he pontificates that Wallace Steven's "imagination even baffles the English reader" (*MP*, 168). And in "The Situation of the American Writer," Spender takes America to task for "lacking a writing and a reading community, prepared to support the best in writing and reading" (*MP*, 187), surely not the case in 1955 and probably not the case now.

Still, *The Making of a Poem* is a group of interesting, informative, sometimes opinionated, often brilliant conversations with a fine mind, one that can articulate truths and validations from a consistent position, such as this: "The problem of every great poet is not just to be great in himself, but to be able to relate his talents to the life of his time, so that he can transform a wide experience of the life of the time into his poetry" (*MP*, 121).

The Struggle of the Modern

After *The Destructive Element* and *The Creative Element*, *The Struggle of the Modern* (1963) is the most highly regarded of Spender's critical work. It is comprised of three rewritten lectures Spender gave in 1961 at the Library of Congress and the completely revised Beckman Lectures he presented at Berkeley in 1959. *The Struggle of the Modern* challenges the tendency of certain reactionary poets, novelists, and critics to surrender up and belittle the free life of the imagination because their integrity is co-opted by conformity, prefabricated intellectualization, and institutional control. The truly modern spirit found expression in the earlier work of Joyce, Eliot, Lawrence, Pound, and Woolf, and in the later poetry of Yeats. These writers and others stimulate Spender's interest because they "show in their work a consciousness of modern art as an aim, whether they accept it or resist it."[10] They treat the experience of modern times as a unity. They use nature and the past to give power to their work. They believe that if art cannot save external society, it can redeem and validate individual human life. The moderns record the changes that have taken place in behavior, thought, discourse, and even manners. They chronicle the evolution of human nature and the alterations in human sensibilities.

> The moderns are therefore those who start off by thinking that human nature has changed: or if not human nature, then the relationship of the individual to the environment, forever being metamorphosized by science, which has altered so completely that there is an effective illusion of change which in fact causes human beings to behave as though they were different. This change, recorded by the seismographic sense of the artist, has also to change all the relations which arrangements of words or marks on canvas which make a poem or novel, or a painting. (*SM*, 13)

Modernists are phoenixes; they rise again and again from the ashes of yesterdays. *The Struggle of the Modern* is a guided tour of literary modernism.

In the early 1960s, Spender also believed, quite correctly as it turned out, that the international modernist movement was breaking up, that its end was inevitable and near, and that energy in literary modernism had flowed from the creative mode to the critical, as evidenced by the brilliance of the New Criticism. "The Modern Movement, in literature at any rate, looks today like past history" (*SM*, 256).

Twentieth-century poets have been overwhelmed by political actions and have lost the innocence of the romantics. They are required to deal with "aesthetic and moral judgements," in other words, truths beyond time-space reality. But timeless values are continually confronted by the exigencies of material existence resulting from "progress." The material benefits of progress, desirable as they are for so many, do not feed the soul. It is only "through the alive intelligence of the imagination" that such benefits "can be related to significant values" (*SM, 58*).

Moving only slightly from Shelley, Spender argues that the poets and creators of today are "separate witnesses, each reflecting his world, and in an interrelationship in which each corrects the vision of the whole. Without them . . . we would not have those voices which express the subjective and spiritual reactions of the most perceptive recording instruments in a civilization" (*SM, 61*).

The Struggle of the Modern, seemingly a clarion call to humanists to save the modernist movement, is really sounding retreat. Too "many contemporaries appear to have deadened themselves, assisted in the deadening by all the machines of advertising and distraction" (*SM, 18*). Mass culture is the worst enemy of art. However, as if undertaking a postmortem prematurely, Spender affirms that the advances of the modernist movement are a permanent addition to the history and the aesthetics of poetry.

The Struggle of the Modern is a complex and difficult book which, however, can at times be exhilarating. Spender tries to accomplish too much: to circumscribe in the largest sense the scope of modernism, to charge the poets of the future, and to educate the critics, especially professors of English literature.

Love-Hate Relations

Love-Hate Relations (1974) began as the Clark Lectures given by Spender at Cambridge University in 1965 but, for publication, were then expanded for beyond the original intentions. The purpose of the book is to explore the constantly changing Anglo-American literary relationship that has obsessed, intrigued, provoked, angered, and amused writers on both sides of the Atlantic from colonial times to the present. The central idea of the book is that Henry James attempted to create a true and permanent Anglo-American literature based in part on common origins and the close literary relationship in the nineteenth century. "For James as a young man, the decision to live in London was . . . crucial, the creative critical act of putting himself at the center of the language and of the solid and stated values which flowed into it."[11] But the American language and American literature went their own ways, and after World War II, British literature grew more concerned with responding to American writing than vice versa. Spender sees a great American advantage in the role of universities as magnetic centers of intellectual life, as patrons of the arts, and as creators of a mass audience.

In the middle of the twentieth century the balance of influence shifted to the Americans. Spender realizes that whereas America once was an extension of European civilization, now Europe is an extension of American civilization. Spender defines European civilization in part as a "continuity of the past tradition" (*LHR,* 310) into the present and future, but for Americans that tradition is more like a museum. Since the future of the world can be expressed in one term, Americanization, Europe will soon regard its cultural past as a collection of artifacts in a museum. American culture is inferior because it has diluted the European tradition. Spender's position is reminiscent of Henry James's attack on the cultural poverty of the United States.

Spender's proposed response by Britain to Americanization is inchoate and not viable. He wants the British to adopt "a studied provincialism, the maintenance of a kind of 'fortress England' " (*LHR,* 318). From the perspective of the 1990s, Spender's literary chauvanism seems almost Victorian. America's fatal attraction for the "orgiastic" and its concern with the intensity of the moment have become the dream, the goal, and now the realization of most of Europe and much of the rest of the world. Spender is right in stating that American energy draws art into the American vortex.

Love-Hate Relations is consistently illuminating. Although not to be compared with D. H. Lawrence's *Studies in Classic American Literature* (1923), it is in the same tradition of growing British fascination with American writing, one of Spender's main points. The satisfaction and pleasure in *Love-Hate Relations* stem from hearing a poet-critic, in elegant language, speak to the world and the future on behalf of literary culture. It is a landmark in Anglo-American literary history.

T. S. Eliot

T. S. Eliot would have been happy with his younger friend's biographical-critical study of him, but for a reason that leaves the work somewhat less interesting to the general reader, for whom it is written, than one might expect, considering that Spender knew Eliot for some 35 years. What is missing is any real attempt to bring Eliot to life through biographical material and personal anecdote. As a study of

Eliot's poetry, drama, and criticism, *T. S. Eliot* (1975) is nevertheless a useful introduction. Generally, Spender is more impressed with Eliot as a poet than as an essayist, and thus, the book is a part of the reevaluation of Eliot as the great literary arbiter of the century. Eliot's "scientific model" of criticism "tends to distract from the poetic behavior it is supposed to describe and focuses the reader on the model itself."[12]

Spender sees Eliot as "obsessed" with poetic drama, as both playwright and critic. Poetic drama could inspire and make meaningful twentieth-century life as it did the Elizabethan Age. Eliot emphasized "that without the spiritual aims set by the Church, modern life is meaningless and empty." But Spender reminds the reader that most of Eliot's contemporaries ignored this view even as they admired plays in which "the true theme is the discovery . . . of . . . religious vocation" (*TSE*, 197). In plays like *Murder in the Cathedral,* the hero is required to perfect his will so that it conforms completely with the will of God. Spender, however, sees will as a tool for individualism, not conformism.

In Spender's consideration, "Little Gidding" of *Four Quartets* is Eliot's masterpiece, partly because in it "the poet had found the true ritual. The word and the Word, the philosophical subject matter and the literally held belief, the mystery which was the religion, and the language which was rich and strange, had . . . become one" (*TSE,* 252). The rest of Eliot's work is an epilogue. There was no last great flowering, as with Yeats, but then few long-lived poets have had one.

Perhaps, after all, T. S. Eliot was not a compatible subject for Spender, despite their long relationship. How could a "devout" atheist be comfortable writing about a poet dedicated to "the idea of a Christian society"?

The Thirties and After: Poetry, Politics, People, 1933–1970

The Thirties and After is a collection of mainly literary essays, reviews, reminiscences, and even poems (collected elsewhere and discussed above) that serve as a kind of informal, intellectual autobiography, tracing Spender's thought decade by decade for almost half a century. It is a wide-ranging cultural potpourri. The book has ghosts walking through it, for Spender's literary essays momentarily bring back to life many of Spender's masters, mentors, and friends: Eliot and Lawrence, Auden and Isherwood, MacNeice and Wyndham Lewis. Spender shows their strengths and weaknesses, their generosity and backbiting. The

political poles of the book are the activism of the 1930s, the reactionaryism of the 1950s, and the negativism of the 1960s. Spender offers
himself as a window on his times. "I myself am, it is only too clear, an
autobiographer."[13] Spender, as always, is totally truthful about himself.
That candor remains a constant cause for admiration.

One highlight of *The Thirties and After* is Spender's plausible explana-
tion of how, when he was editor of *Encounter,* he was hoodwinked by the
CIA. A group of 40 different American foundations and a rich American financier seemed to be funding the distinguished publication. It
turned out that one foundation was the main source of funding and it
was a front for the CIA (*TA,* 128). Spender knew nothing of this until
it was revealed in 1967. The CIA never managed to, or apparently even
attempted to, influence editorial decision. One wonders why the
agency was doing it? In looking back on his writing for *Encounter,*
Spender believes that his best contributions were sections of his journals
(*TA,* 129).

Spender's reminiscence of Eliot is delicate and respectful, although
he admits that "Yeats might be 'greater' " (*TA,* 129). And although
Spender could never accept Eliot's reactionaryism, he is genuinely glad
that his old patron found happiness in the last eight years of his life
through his second marriage.

Auden will forever remain, for Spender, "the tow-haired undergraduate poet with the abruptly turning head, and eyes that quickly take the
measure of people and ideas" (*TA,* 228). In the end, after the defections
and the deaths of the friends of his youth, Spender, the steadfast one,
who braved out the war, who admitted mistakes, who continued to
trust, who stayed ingenuous, remains the custodian of the past. That
function is exercised in *The Thirties and After.*

Of the major thirties writers, Spender, the sole survivor, had, and
has, the sharpest critical intellect. He has made by far the most significant contribution to the care and feeding of twentieth-century literature. Spender's very life is literary history, but his criticism will have a
life of its own. It is important because it speaks boldly and truly,
because it is restrained and just, because it is encompassing and pene-
trating, because it is a viable defense of literary culture, and because it
is auxiliary and pertinent to a major poet's work.

Chapter Six
A Personal Approach: Politics and Social History

Stephen Spender's entire career has had its political overtones and undercurrents. After all, there are not many writers who have been called a tool of Stalin and an agent of the CIA. Spender has frequently been attacked by the Left and the Right—and at the same time! He was probably a fully committed Communist for about five weeks. Although his politics have gradually moved right, he has remained left of center. Today he is on the editorial board, and continues to write for, *Granta,* a periodical devoted to supporting the freedom of writers everywhere.

Like his approach to literary criticism, Spender's approach to politics is personalistic. He has continually tried to adjust to sociopolitical events as a humanist. When political force impinges on individual rights he goes to the barricades.

Forward from Liberalism

A 1937 selection of the New Left Book Club, *Forward from Liberalism* records the uncertainties in Spender's attempt to find and support a position left of liberalism, the political creed he was born to. The central argument of *Forward from Liberalism* is that liberals must reconcile Communists' regard for social justice with their regard for social freedom, and they must accept communist methods necessary to defeat fascism, because those methods are the only hope. Spender describes the experiences that led him to this belief, he explores the historical reasons for the failure of liberalism, and he also examines his own doubts concerning communism. Lastly, he conjectures that individuals no longer can influence history for the better unless they unite with a larger entity: "The nature of the revolution which we make, the liberty and equality of the new society, the socialist example set before the world, depend largely on our willingness to act soon and to combine with those whose final aims are the peace and liberty identical with our own."[1]

In the final analysis, the only integrity is personal integrity. Spender knows that although it may be correct for a group to demand loyalty from an individual, it is wrong to try to transform his or her mind into a group mind. For its time *Forward from Liberalism* is a wise book from an honest and bright young man. Although Spender urges British society to go forward from liberalism, he desires it to bring along the best of liberal values on the journey to necessity. The Communists were not really happy with *Forward from Liberalism,* but then Spender, Auden, Day Lewis, and MacNeice were continually "struggling with the views of the side they were supporting" (*CE,* 153).

Citizens in War—and After

As a fireman in wartime London, Spender quickly became aware of the price civilian populations have to pay in international conflicts. *Citizens in War—and After* (1945) illustrates the results of the Blitz, and the people, training, and methods used to keep casualties at a minimum, care for the wounded, and permit a city to carry on. The thesis, that Civil Defense is the responsibility of all citizens, is established and supported to a large extent by 48 dramatic, colored photographs.

Citizens in War—and After salutes the brave members of the National Fire Service and the auxiliary workers such as ambulance crews and first aid parties in factories. The survival of the people is in their own hands. Spender wants his country ready for passive defense if unfortunately there should be the need once more. Civilian Defense training is really a matter for peacetime. In war it may be too late. This is, of course, a pre-nuclear weapons position.

"Stephen Spender" in *The God That Failed*

One of the most important books of the cold war, published in 1949 soon after its inception, is *The God That Failed,* edited by Richard Crossman. In it "six intellectuals describe their journey into communism and the return."[2] They are Arthur Koestler, Ignazio Silone, Richard Wright, André Gide, Louis Fischer, and Stephen Spender. A search for a way to better humanity's lot had led them to communism. What they saw, what they experienced, and what they were expected to do led them to revulsion, personal agony, disillusionment, and finally rejection of communism. Crossman's book, stemming from a conversation with Koestler, became a major contribution to an understanding by other intellectuals and scholars of the dimensions and depths of communism. Spender's essay, a frank confession of naïveté and quick disillusionment, has been considered the most salient of the essays, partly because of the effective writing and partly because it is directed at artists. Its placement at the end of the book is evidence of its special significance.

Most unforgettable for Spender was the communist attempt to control the minds and the production of artists: "To say that an artist is an individualist is not to say that he creates only out of himself only for himself. It is to say that he creates out of a level of his own experiences, which has profound connections with the experiences of many people on a level where they are not just expressions of social needs. . . . To make individual experience submit to the generalization of official information and observation, is to cut humanity off from a main means of becoming conscious of itself as a community of individuals existing together within many separate personal lives" (*GF,* 270–71). The death of freedom cannot be "justified by a slogan: that freedom is a recognition of necessity" (*GF,* 271). Humans are not to be turned into machines for the altering of society.

Spender could never bring himself to hate capitalism, nor could any person or group convert him to such a hatred. Indeed, Spender simply cannot hate. He had learned that the personal sense of social guilt that had caused him to take sides could not cause him to abandon his ideals of individualism and artistic freedom. To give up his individuality was to give up his soul. Spender's essay has been a guide to troubled artistic consciences for more than 40 years.

The Year of the Young Rebels

In 1968 the universities of the West burst into rebellion. Spender set out to find the underlying causes of this revolt. There could hardly have been a better person to do this job and to write *The Year of the Young Rebels* (1969). Nearly 70, Spender, who had once been a student radical and a dropout from Oxford, had the wisdom, experience, and sensitivity to do justice to the students and their causes.

The Year of the Young Rebels is a collection of essays depicting and commenting on the student battles at Columbia, the Sorbonne, and universities in Prague and Berlin. Spender tries to establish the significance for the world of the youth revolt and to position it in a changing culture. The last three chapters collate the experiences West and East, show their similarities and differences, and defend the students from many of their detractors in the university establishment.

At Columbia, Spender saw the difference between the actions of the undisciplined, variously motivated white activists and the well-organized black students, who had a clear agenda. They were like "diplomats . . . on the point of breaking off relations with another power."[3] Indeed, they became an independent power. When they were in position, they asked their white comrades to get out of the way. They achieved changes still in operation today: an African-American studies program, more black history and culture in the general curriculum, and black faculty teaching black students. In essence "a new kind of segregation," one that would allow African-American students time and space and a chance to develop their own cultural destiny.

The French students at the Sorbonne were different. For them and their predecessors conflict with authority was a way of life: "They equate revolution with spontaneity, participation, communication, imagination, love, youth. Relations between the students and young workers who share—or who are converted to—these values are of the first importance. They dramatise a struggle not so much between proletarian and capitalist materialism as between forces of life and the dead oppressive weight of the bourgeoisie. They are against the consumer society, paternalism, bureaucracy, impersonal party progress, and static party hierarchies. Revolution must not become ossified. It is *la révolution permanente*" (*YYR*, 45). But because they were obdurate and unself-critical, their poorly disguised bourgeois values antagonized the workers, who refused to join them. Thus, Charles de Gaulle survived and they failed.

Spender is happiest with, and proudest of, the Czech students, who were fighting for the things the Western students took for granted: books, light, more classes, and, most of all, academic freedom. The students of the West who wished to revolutionize their society but began by first trying to destroy their university seemed like an army opening warfare by burning its own base. "For the university, even if it does not conform to their wishes, is an arsenal from which they can draw the arms which can change society" (*YYR*, 57).

Spender's sagacious program for activist students and their vast energy calls for them to take on the problems of the world: the brainwashing of the young, the population bomb, "the destruction of nature and animal life." They have the "prerequisite existential awareness" and the "feeling that they incarnate the sense of life" (*YYR*, 185). The advice remains valid and timely.

Stephen Spender was witness to the two periods in the history of the twentieth century in the West when capitalism was shaken: the Great Depression of the 1930s and the student revolutions of 1968. During the first upheaval, Spender contributed a manifesto, *Forward from Liberalism*, and was an activist writer in the movement for change. In 1968, Spender was a Thucydides, recording and interpreting events in *The Year of the Young Rebels*. Capitalism survived the trials of the century. Communism did not. Spender, so much the archetypal twentieth-century artist, has accepted the decisions of history with wisdom and grace. He has absorbed hard lessons and shared his understanding with us all.

Chapter Seven

Within Other Worlds: Miscellaneous Writing

Stephen Spender's output is enormous. Hardly a genre or subgenre exists at which he has not tried his hand. Many readers over the decades have come to know Spender's writing through genres other than poetry. Reader's of biography quickly appreciated the insights and candor of his early autobiography, *World within World,* and have been interested in his journals and published letters, for they are important chronicles of the history and the art of the century. Other readers have first engaged with Spender by reading about his experiences in, and observations on, the ravaged European continent directly after World War II, or his journey to Israel shortly after the state's founding. The conspicuous characteristics of Spender's nonfiction, noncritical prose are clarity and probity.

Autobiography, Journals, and Letters

Auden commented on it. Spender has sometimes allowed it. He has a primary talent for autobiography. The poetry and the fiction sing the song of himself. Perhaps referring to Spender's over six-foot height, William York Tyndall calls *World within World* "the tallest memorial to the Auden period."[1]

World within World Even though Spender claims to be "mainly concerned with a few themes: love, poets, politics, the life of literature, childhood, travel, and the development of certain attitudes towards moral problems" (*WW,* v), *World within World* is a very good handbook to the cultural history of the 1930s and early 1940s and to the relationship between literature and politics in that era. Literary critics and biographers continually consult *World within World* for its close-up portraits of Yeats, Eliot, Woolf, Auden, Malraux, the three Sitwells, Cyril Connolly, Isherwood, Day Lewis, and others. Historians have valued Spender's insights into, and explanations of, the motives that led so many well-educated, privileged artists of Spender's generation into social activism and leftist politics and then disillusionment. *World within World* is also a part of the history of the Spanish Civil War, as seen by an Englishman of the Left.

Spender wrote *World within World* as he was passing 40, a time when people are wont to look back a bit on their perhaps half-completed lives and wonder where they have been, where they are, and where they are going? They also contemplate the "meaning" of their lives. Spender goes further; he is concerned with the meaning of individual life itself, especially an artist's life, in light of the events of the first half of the twentieth century: incredibly destructive wars, collectivization, the lockstep "isms," the end of empires, the massive world population increase, the Holocaust, and the dehumanization of art. He chooses to examine his own life as a disquisition on positing "self" in a quicksand world.

The structure of the autobiography, which reads much like a confessional novel, is somewhat awkward because Spender believes that the convention of having an autobiography begin with a detailed account of childhood is a cliché and ill advised, since readers really want to learn about the accomplishments of a life, and so he begins the book from a backward-looking perspective of 19, proceeds to discuss his life to age 40, and then adds 12 pages to the fifth section of the book, just after talking about the Blitz, to discuss his early childhood in detail. Thus, *World within World* moves in a circular fashion, recounting childhood. Surely it would have been better for the reader to leave the experience of the book with Spender's artistic and personal achievements more freshly in mind than a remembrance of unhappy days at school.

The candor of *World within World* is remarkable, especially considering the year of publication. Spender reveals all without mitigation, especially his own political and sexual ambivalences. He describes his sense of alienation at Oxford and how erratically he worked as a student. Spender was dominated by emotions. Less mature than most of his schoolmates, he wanted desperately to please. He fell in love with them too easily. The outstanding acquaintances at Oxford were gifted young men with whom he would remain friends for life—Auden, MacNeice, and Bernard Spencer, for example. But his deepest feelings were reserved for homosexual relationships and crushes like that with pseudonymous Marston. Spender also tried to make friends with young women and desired heterosexual relationships, but he had grown up in a puritanical home and an all-male school system.

Spender candidly discusses the difficulty he had as an adolescent getting used to the idea that he was part Jewish: "That we were of Jewish as well as German origin was passed over in silence or with slight embarrassment by my family" (*WW,* 11). He also is frank about the sexual attractions of Weimar Germany that led him to drop out of Oxford before taking a degree and taste the exotic life of Berlin and Hamburg.

Spender's relationship with his father was a troubled one, and it is not resolved in *World within World,* ever after the older man's death. Spender's portrait of Harold Spender is flavored with subtle dislike and resentment. At this time, Spender begins to deal with his guilt over his class privilege, for Oxford, Auden, and life had sensitized him to the reality of economic and social injustice and inequity. He strongly believes in the overriding importance of the freedom of the individual, but his communist friends told him that his "sense of freedom was only a projection of the interest of the bourgeois class" (*WW,* 124). He learned that guilt "may create a stumbling darkness in which we cannot act," but it may also provide a thread leading us "out of a labyrinth, into places where we accept . . . the responsibilty of action" (*WW,* 125).

The autobiography shows how Spender ascended rocketlike to fame as a poet in only five years. Indeed, it is difficult to find a multigenre literary success story in the 1930s to parallel Spender's. But Spender's personal life at the time was counterposed to his professional life. His first marriage failed and he was miserable. Again he tells all. Fortunately, his second marriage succeeded.

The fourth and fifth sections of *World within World* are as interesting as the earlier Oxford-Germany sections. The fourth recounts Spender's Spanish Civil War involvement and the personal activities of English and other European intellectuals in aid of the doomed cause of the Spanish Republic. The fifth describes the aftermath, in particular World War II and the dangers of work in the National Fire Service during the bombing of London.

It is difficult to put down *World within World* once one has started to read it, because of the author's ability to vivify the people and events of his early life. The pleasures and pains are palpable. Spender's personality shines through in such a way that it is impossible not to like him very much. As to the meaning of life? It seems to reside in simply getting about the business of living and writing.

Letters to Christopher   Spender met Christopher Isherwood, a Cambridge man, through their friend Auden. They became lovers and then lifelong friends, despite occasional rifts, after which Spender was always willing and glad to make up. *Letters to Christopher* consists of 42 letters written to Isherwood between 1929 and 1939, and two journal entries, one from 1931 relating a month's journey in Spain and the other describing the events in Spender's and Britain's lives from the outbreak of war in September 1939 through November.

The letters begin as naive and immature confessions of love, hero worship (Isherwood was five years older), jealousy, and crushes on other youths, while coincidentally portraying the life of an Oxford undergraduate. Fortunately, fragments of experiments in writing began to appear, making for some interest besides the gossip. And then the letters begin to tell of publishing successes, a growing literary reputation for Spender, meetings with Eliot, Forster, and Virginia and Leonard Woolf. But Spender also expresses his sexual confusion, and the friends fall out and reconcile. Early versions of important poems appear, and then Spender is writing from the war in Spain. He tells of the betrayal by his wife Inez, and both Isherwood and Auden offer comfort. Spender cannot bear to be left: "I have always loved people in the manner of thinking that they were indispensable to me and of becoming completely absorbed in their personalities."[2]

The letters evolve into sophisticated comments on the rise of fascism, the capitals of Europe, political commitments, the London literary scene, and the coming of war. They reveal a journey of maturation and intellectual growth, of aesthetic development and the mastering of emotions, of the passage from self-love to world love, until in 1939 Spender could say, "The world should be home, it should be somewhere everyone has his place, is surrounded by simple machinery, the task, the house, the furniture, the companion, the river, the trees or the streets which assure him that he is loved" (*LC,* 191).

Letters to Christopher is important primary material for the study of the literature and politics of the 1930s as well as for understanding Spender's development as a major poet in the pre–World War II period. It would have been both useful and pleasurable to have had Isherwood's replies.

Journals, 1939–1983   Stephen Spender had John Goldsmith select some five hundred pages of journal entries ranging from 3 September 1939 (the day Great Britain declared war on Germany) to 29 May 1983. Small portions of the journal had previously been published in *Encounter* and *Letters to Christopher.* The material is divided into 12 sections each prefaced by Spender with a short background essay. These essays alone form an excellent sketch of twentieth-century British literary history and, together with the journal entries, constitute another autobiography. *Journals, 1939–1983* (1986) and *Collected Poems, 1928– 1985* were published almost simultaneously. They are Spender's self-chiseled monument, front and back.

Again Spender's total and often painful candor shines through the earlier portions, but then with time, fame, and worldliness, the writing grows self-conscious and turns to accounting conferences, receptions, powerful and famous acquaintances, literary and celebrity gossip, and international cultural missionary work. Spender's friends in the *Journals* are the legion of power and the honor role of art: the Queen Mother, the Archbishop of Canterbury, Baron Philip de Rothschild, Lady Astor, Jacqueline Kennedy Onassis, Henry Moore, Ezra Pound, Edith Sitwell, Sir Isaiah Berlin, Francis Bacon, Harold Pinter, Joan Littlewood, Peggy Ashcroft, George Kennan, Robert Lowell, Alan Tate, Susan Sontag, Allen Ginsberg, Mary McCarthy, and of course, Woolf, Eliot, Auden, Isherwood, MacNeice, and Day Lewis.

Clearly, however, Spender never developed a mammoth ego. Indeed, his self-effacement may have even hindered the growth of his literary reputation. The *Journals* show that unlike most other major poets of the century he remained open and flexible in regard to evolving political and social ideas, the changing problems and solutions of the cold war era, and the dangers of national interest in the Nuclear Age. It is an oversimplification, but this Oxford-educated son of privilege, who eventually traveled in the Concorde set, remained politically decent and proletarian in sentiment.

Travel Books

It is ironic that of Spender's three travel books the first is about Germany and the second about Israel. Spender went to Germany in 1945 just after the war's end to see what was left of the German high culture he had loved and admired before Hitler and "to inquire into the lives and ideas of German intellectuals, with a particular view to discovering any surviving talent in German literature."[3] He went to Israel at the invitation of Youth Aliyah, a Zionist organization caring for sixty thousand children, mostly orphans who escaped the German policy of racial murder. His overriding interest was the country. "To study the children is to study the germ of the New State."[4]

European Witness During late 1945, Spender kept careful journals of his experiences visiting the British-occupied zone of Germany. He also visited France, which was recovering from the German occupation and the destructive course of armies. All in all, he spent about five months on the Continent as "a European witness." Although ostensibly trying to ascertain the damage to intellectual life that the Nazis and the war had caused, he also wanted to meet displaced persons, to see and comprehend the concentration camps, and to note the effect of victory and occupation duty on the British army. Additionally, there was surely an underlying motivation. Like so many European and American intellectuals, he wished to understand aspects of the German character, which could be artistic and sentimental, yet simultaneously kill in cold blood innocent men, women, and children with "apparent lack of feeling," murmuring "*Pflicht ist Pflicht,* Duty is Duty" (*EW,* 4).

Spender is an acute observer, and *European Witness* is good reporting. He is also patient, a good listener, understanding, and forgiving. Instinctively, he knows that the Germans, like other people, must be treated as individual human beings, and that after war, winners as well as losers face trials. With his liberal optimism, he hopes that they will grow together and grow better with time. They did.

Spender's only contempt is directed at the former Nazi leaders like Hitler and Joseph Goebbels, because not only did they destroy much of Europe but they also killed culture. They were assassins of art, beauty, grace, and the human spirit. "The cities and soil of Germany where they were sacrificed were not just places of material destruction. They were altars on which a solemn sacrifice had been prepared. . . . The whold world had seemed to be darkened with their darkness, and when they left the world, the threat of a still greater darkness, a total and everlasting one, rose up from their ashes" (*EW,* 245–246).

Fittingly, Spender ends *European Witness* in Berlin, a city that he had loved in his youth, where Isherwood had introduced him to bright thoughts and dark practices, where "tradition was a caricature and a mockery, where action was conceived of entirely in terms of power" (*EW,* 226), and that, at this writing, is about to become once more the cultural and political capital of Germany.

Learning Laughter   Spender traveled to Israel on a "children's boat," a ship of orphans, from Marseilles to Haifa. It could only have been a poignant experience, but once in Israel he became aware of, and particularly interested in, the problems of the young country, a democracy in a sea of despotism, a tiny land unable to find peace with hating neighbors.

Spender, however, is as critical as admiring. He foresaw current antagonism between Jews of Western origin and those of "Oriental" background. Could they, and could the secular and the extreme orthodox, ever reconcile? Could their religious and cultural tenets be strong enough to bridge the chasm of distrust? But he concluded that although "there is a widespread feeling of discouragement in the young State four years after its birth," nevertheless "there are no signs of the nation falling apart" (*LL, 198*).

The Holy Land has a great potential for tranquility, Spender concludes. He knows that the small nation's ideals came from the liberal and socialist revolutionary movement of Russia before Stalin. The kibbutz is a place of sharing, of community ownership and responsibility, a place where culture takes precedence over commerce. *Learning Laughter* is ultimately about ingathering and friendship. The fundamental idealism of Israel may yet rise to regional reconciliation.

China Diary   Spender and the artist David Hockney flew to China in May 1981 to observe, write, photograph, draw, and paint their impressions of that country on the commission of the London publishers Thames and Hudson for the purpose of producing a large-format book on China. They began in Hong Kong and then journeyed to Beijing, Xian, Nanjing, Hangzhou, Wuxi, Shanghai, and Canton. Spender took notes while Hockney photographed and sketched. They were accompanied by official government guides everywhere. They did all the tourist things and met few Chinese people. Most of the three weeks in China were spent sightseeing and seeking photo opportunities.

Spender's commentary is genial and typically self-effacing. The artwork, 158 paintings, sketches, and photographs, happily avoids the travel brochure clichés. *China Diary* provides aesthetic pleasure and some insight into what post–Cultural Revolution China was like before the repression of 1989.

Chapter Eight
Spender's Achievement

As a young poet in the 1930s, Stephen Spender earned a reputation as a radical writer of concern, addressing the politically conscience-striken Left of his time. He wrote poetry with a program. Along with others, he wanted to absorb the modern technology of the machine into a "new writing" that rejected Georgian pastoralism and lyricism; admired but did not fully emulate the pessimistic, mythopoeic, less accessible poetry of Pound and Eliot; and strove to change, perhaps save, a seemingly moribund society by whipping flaccid liberals into a more radical mode, in order to change Fabians into Communists and to beat market shares into plowshares. The modernists envisioned a spiritual technology, but they failed to make their revolution, and communism failed them. They retreated and dispersed. Auden and Spender, the Wordsworth and Coleridge of their time, abandoned the cause, drifted to the right, and recoiled into themselves. Like MacNeice and Day Lewis, they did leave a significant body of poetry in the wake of their lives, of which Spender's is the most personal, sensitive, and compassionate.

The anthology poems "Not Palaces, an Era's Crown," "I think continually of those who were truly great," "The Express," "The Landscape near Aerodrome," and "Ultima Ratio Regum" are among the most memorable of the 1930s, for they authentically express the best values and the most painful tensions of that troubled time. With Auden's departure to America in 1939, Spender became the leading young British writer of lyric poetry and liberal politics. He was the bridge between pre–World War II modernism and all that came after.

The Struggle

Almost from the beginning, Spender tried "redeeming the world by introspection."[1] The struggle of the inner world with the outer, which MacNeice treats lightly, is the very essence of Spender's modernism. He posited himself between two worlds. In *The Creative Element* he opines that one has to look beyond the distinction between an external world which is "real" and an inwardness supposedly "unreal." One has to ask what, in a world that is "spiritually barren," can the real attitude of the inner life towards external things be? Significant reality is, surely, a balanced relationship between outer and inner worlds. The inner world of a writer may become incommunicable, but in a time when the external world has become "spiritually barren" outer reality is only real in the sense of being factual. The result of that excessive outwardness of a "spiritually barren external world" is the "excessive inwardness" of poets who prefer losing themselves within themselves to losing themselves outside themselves in external reality. (*CE*, 21)

Thus, like Rilke, Spender is deeply aware of, and disturbed by, the pressure of the outer world on the inner life. The physical world disappointed Spender. It did seem "spiritually barren." Thus, "writings are my only wings away" (*CP* 1955, 21).

Spender has searched for a rational system of belief. He has wanted to understand existence, to deny the death wish in the world and in himself, and to find harmony. He achieved some of these goals, but in the course of the quest he came to know that it is in process that meaning may be found.

From the 1940s on, with the failure of both liberalism and socialism to stop fascism from attempting world conquest, with the horrors of World War II and the errors of the cold war, Spender grew increasingly disillusioned with political action and even the efficacy of art. His poetry became less topical and more personal. Subjective experience became a microcosm of all the world he cared to know. Simultaneously, his recognition and esteem as a critic rose. With time and age he became a "witness," one who had seen and lived history.

Influence

Spender's influence on younger writers has not been much noticed. As a lionized writer, a respected critic, an important player in cultural politics, and a university lecturer, he was much read, observed, respected, and emulated by practicing poets. Dylan Thomas, with all the dazzling language, found license for his subjectivity in Spender's exploration of "I." And Spender gave Thomas encouragement and arranged for publication in, and payment by, *Horizon* in the 1940s. Philip Larkin, an Oxford man, distilled the essence of the ordinary scene, the trivial moment, and the life of the town in ways not dissimilar to early Spender.

Poems of Charles Tomlinson, like "The Crane," are echoes of Spender's machinery pieces. Ted Hughes's *Hawk in the Rain* emotional and physical manner derives in part from Spender's sensual first poems. Spender's *Collected Poems, 1928–1953* came out in 1955, while Hughes was studying at Cambridge. It was eagerly read by the younger generation of poets. "Seamus Heaney's career reflects a tension between impersonal and personal views of poetry not unlike that marking the work of Stephen Spender and C. Day Lewis in the late 1930s."[2]

The Artist as Humanist

Today Stephen Spender is in his eighties, but he is as young as Shelley. Although his reputation as a poet has fallen, it will be resurrected in time and accorded a high place in the history of twentieth-century British literature. George Orwell said, "There is no test of literary merit except survival." Spender has his passport to Parnassus.

Spender is part of that long tradition of romantic poets, beginning really with Shelley, who believes that there is more to art than individualism. Poetry is not only self-expression. There is craft and there is service. There is compassion and engagement. But never at the price of freedom and the artist's right to create as he or she wills. The goal was, and is, as Samuel Hynes says, "a Good Society in which individuals might flourish."[3] The poet's responsibility to the world is to realize in concrete images personal feelings and experiences of significance to the public, because those images can affect history. Poetry thus validates individualism because that individualism serves society.

Spender's most important contribution may be that as a humanist artist living through troubled times he used his talents and energies to help us and himself understand a world we did not create, but one he finally accepted and tried to improve, while other artists escaped totally to closed inner worlds of myths and dreams, to religion, or to history. He faced the dilemma of the moral, socially responsible human being in a world of irreconcilable differences. Therein lies Spender's authority. Those are his credentials.

Notes and References

Chapter One

1. *World within World* (New York: Harcourt, Brace, 1951), 11; hereafter cited in the text as *WW*.
2. Charles Osborne, *W. H. Auden: The Life of a Poet* (New York: Harcourt Brace Jovanovich, 1979), 52.
3. Christopher Isherwood, *Lions and Shadows* (Norfolk, Conn.: New Direction, 1947), 282, 303.
4. H. B. Kulkarni, *Stephen Spender: Poet in Crisis* (Bombay: Blackie, 1970), 16.
5. Louis MacNeice, *The Strings Are False* (London: Faber and Faber, 1965), 113–14.
6. William York Tindall, *Forces in Modern British Literature, 1885–1956* (New York: Vintage, 1956), 43.
7. Virginia Woolf, "A Letter to a Young Poet," *The Death of a Moth and Other Essays* (New York: Harcourt, Brace, 1942), 224.
8. See Valentine Cunningham, *British Writers of the Thirties* (New York: Oxford, 1988), 148.
9. *Journals, 1939–1983* (New York: Random House, 1986), 21; hereafter cited in the text as *J*.
10. Norman Sherry, *The Life of Graham Greene I, 1904–1939* (New York: Viking, 1989), 607.
11. V. S. Pritchard, "Books in General," *New Statesman and Nation,* 14 April 1951, 426.
12. Geoffrey Thurley, "A Kind of Scapegoat: A Retrospective on Stephen Spender," *The Ironic Harvest: English Poetry in the Twentieth Century* (London: Edward Arnold, 1974), 79.
13. Blake Morrison, "Young Poets in the 1970s," *British Poetry since 1970: A Critical Survey,* eds. Peter Jones and Michael Schmidt (New York: Persea, 1980), 142–43.
14. Introduction to H. B. Kulkarni, *Stephen Spender, Works and Criticism: An Annotated Bibliography* (New York: Garland, 1976), ix.
15. Cynthia Ozick, "T. S. Eliot at 101," *New Yorker,* 20 November 1989, 154.

Chapter Two

1. Justin Replogle, "The Auden Group," *Wisconsin Studies in Contemporary Literature* 5 (1964), 136.

2. Michael Roberts, ed., *New Signatures* (London: Hogarth Press, 1932), 12; hereafter cited in the text as *NS*.

3. A Kingley Weatherhead, *Stephen Spender and the Thirties* (Lewisburg, Pa.: Bucknell University Press, 1975), 221.

4. Francis Scarfe, "Stephen Spender: A Sensitive," *Auden and After: The Liberation of Poetry, 1930–1941* (London: Routledge, 1942), 35.

5. Thurley, "A Kind of Scapegoat," 79.

6. *Nine Experiments* (Hampstead: privately printed, 1928; facsimile repr., Elliston Poetry Foundation, University of Cincinnati, 1964), 13; hereafter cited in the text as *NE*.

7. Louis Untermeyer, "Poetry of Power," *Saturday Review of Literature,* 10 November 1934, 274.

8. G. S. Fraser, *Vision and Rhetoric* (London: Faber and Faber, 1959), 205.

9. *Twenty Poems* (London: Blackwell, 1930), 2; hereafter cited in the text as *TP*.

10. Elton Edward Smith, "Stephen Spender, the Proletarian Poet," *The Angry Young Men of the Thirties* (Carbondale: Southern Illinois University Press, 1975), 65.

11. See Paul Fussell, *The Great War and Modern Memory* (London: Oxford University Press, 1975), 279–86.

12. D. E. S. Maxwell, *Poets of the Thirties* (London: Routledge and Kegan Paul, 1969), 196.

13. Osborne, *W. H. Auden,* 96.

14. Fraser, *Vision and Rhetoric,* 207–8.

15. Morton Zabel, "The Purpose of Stephen Spender," *Poetry* 45, no. 4 (January 1935), 209.

16. Thurley, "A Kind of Scapegoat," 81.

17. *Poems,* 2nd ed. (New York: Random House, 1934), 57; hereafter cited in the text as *P*.

18. James Southworth, "Stephen Spender," *Sewanee Review* 45 (July 1937), 275.

19. MacNeice, *The Strings Are False,* 128.

20. Samuel Hynes, *The Auden Generation* (New York: Viking, 1972), 67.

21. Replogle, "The Auden Group," 139.

22. Morton Seif, "The Impact of T. S. Eliot on Auden and Spender," *South Atlantic Quarterly* 53 (January 1954), 62.

23. *Vienna* (New York: Random House, 1935), 10; hereafter cited in the text as *V*.

24. Hynes, *The Auden Generation,* 145.

25. *The Still Centre* (London: Faber and Faber, 1939), 11; hereafter cited in the text as *SC*.

26. David Daiches, *Poetry and the Modern World* (Chicago: University of Chicago Press, 1940), 237.

27. Robert D. Harper, "Back to the Personal," *Poetry* 57 (October 1940), 49.

28. "Inside the Cage," *The Making of a Poet* (London: Hamish Hamilton, 1955), 15.

29. C. Day Lewis, *A Hope for Poetry* (Oxford: Basil Blackwell, 1934), 95.

30. Introduction, *Collected Poems, 1928–1953* (New York: Random House, 1955), xvi.

31. A. T. Tolley, *The Poetry of the Thirties* (London: Victor Gollancz, 1975), 352.

32. Preface to *The Collected Poems of Wilfred Owen,* ed. C. Day Lewis (London: Chatto and Windus, 1963), 31.

33. Hynes, *The Auden Generation,* 251.

34. Hugh D. Ford, *A Poet's War: British Poets and the Spanish Civil War* (Philadelphia: University of Pennsylvania Press, 1965), 232.

35. Cyril Connolly, "Today the Struggle," *New Statesman and Nation,* 5 June 1937, 926.

36. Katherine Bail Hoskins, *Today the Struggle: Literature and Politics in England during the Spanish Civil War* (Austin: University of Texas Press, 1969), 227.

37. Cunningham, *British Writers of the Thirties,* 199.

38. Harper, "Back to the Personal," 49.

Chapter Three

1. "Poetry and Revolution," *New Country: Prose and Poetry by the Authors of New Signatures,* ed. Michael Roberts (London: Hogarth Press, 1933), 62; hereafter cited in the text as *NC.*

2. *Poetry since 1939* (London: Longmans, Green, 1946), 34; hereafter cited in the text as *PS39.*

3. John Press, *A Map of Modern English Verse* (London: Oxford University Press, 1969), 232.

4. *Ruins and Visions* (London: Faber and Faber, 1942), 11; hereafter cited in the text as *RV.*

5. Daiches, *Poetry and the Modern World,* 241.

6. Thurley, "A Kind of Scapegoat," 95.

7. Louis MacNeice, *Modern Poetry* (London: Oxford University Press, [1938] 1968), 106.

8. "The Imagination as Verb," *The Imagination in the Modern World* (Washington, D.C.: Library of Congress, 1962), 9.

9. *Poems of Dedication* (New York: Random House, 1947), 11; hereafter cited in the text as *PD.*

10. *The Edge of Being* (New York: Random House, 1949), 9; hereafter cited in the text as *EB.*

11. A. T. Tolley, *The Poetry of the Forties* (Ottawa: Carleton University Press, 1985), 279.

12. *Collected Poems, 1928–1953* (New York: Random House, 1955), xvii; hereafter cited in the text as *CP* 1955.

13. Fraser, *Vision and Rhetoric,* 209.

14. *Selected Poems* (New York: Random House, 1964), vii; hereafter cited in the text as *SP.*

15. *The Generous Days,* 2nd ed. (New York: Random House, 1971), 45; hereafter cited in the text as *GD.*

16. Victor Howes, "Concern for Change," *Christian Science Monitor,* 2 December 1971, 29.

17. *Recent Poems* (London: Anvil Press, 1978), pages unnumbered (4); hereafter cited in the text as RP.

18. *Collected Poems, 1928–1985* (New York: Random House, 1986), 13; hereafter cited in the text as *CP* 1986.

19. Osborne, *W. H. Auden,* 308.

20. F. R. Leavis, *New Bearings in English Poetry* (Ann Arbor: University of Michigan Press, 1960), 234.

21. A. K. Weatherhead, "Stephen Spender: Lyric Impulse and Will," *Contemporary Literature* 12 (Autumn 1971), 451.

Chapter Four

1. *The Backward Son* (London: Hogarth Press, 1940), 138; hereafter cited in the text as *BS.*

2. John Lehmann, *I Am My Brother* (New York: Reynal, 1960), 32.

3. *The Temple* (New York: Grove Press, 1988), x; hereafter cited in the text as *T.*

4. *The Burning Cactus* (New York: Random House, 1936), 17; hereafter cited in the text as *BC.*

5. Graham Greene, "Legend," *Spectator,* 24 April 1936, 766.

6. Maxwell, *Poets of the Thirties,* 192.

7. *Engaged in Writing, and The Fool and the Princess* (New York: Farrar, Straus and Cudahy, 1958), 107; hereafter cited in the text as *EW.*

8. Julian Symons, *The Thirties: A Dream Relived* (London: Cresset, 1960), 86.

9. "Poetry and Expressionism," *New Statesman and Nation,* 12 March 1938, 408.

10. *Trial of a Judge* (New York: Random House, 1938), 13; hereafter cited in the text as *TJ.*

Chapter Five

1. Hynes, *The Auden Generation,* 104.

2. I. A. Richards, *Science and Poetry* (London: Kegan Paul, Trench, Trubner, 1926), 65.

3. *The Destructive Element* (Philadelphia: Albert Saifer, 1953), 14; hereafter cited in the text as *DE.*

4. *The New Realism: A Discussion* (London: Hogarth Press, 1939), 5; hereafter cited in the text as *NR*.

5. Hynes, *The Auden Generation,* 362.

6. *Life and the Poet* (New York: Haskell House, 1974), 24; hereafter cited in the text as *LP*.

7. Alfred North Whitehead, *Science and the Modern World* (New York: New American Library, 1948), 105.

8. *The Creative Element* (London: Hamish Hamilton, 1953), 11; hereafter cited in the text as *CE*.

9. *The Making of a Poem* (London: Hamish Hamilton, 1955), 9; hereafter cited in the text as *MP*.

10. *The Struggle of the Modern* (Berkeley and Los Angeles: University of California Press, 1963), x; hereafter cited in the text as *SM*.

11. *Love-Hate Relations* (New York: Random House, 1974), 87; hereafter cited in the text as *LHR*.

12. *T. S. Eliot* (New York: Viking, 1975), 72; hereafter cited in the text as *TSE*.

13. *The Thirties and After: Poetry, Politics, People 1933–1970* (New York: Random House, 1978), 235; hereafter cited in the text as *TA*.

Chapter Six

1. *Forward from Liberalism* (London: Victor Gollancz, 1937), 295.

2. Richard Crossman, ed., *The God That Failed* (New York: Harper, 1949), 3; hereafter cited in the text as *GF*.

3. *The Year of the Young Rebels* (New York: Random House, 1969), 32; hereafter cited in the text as *YYR*.

Chapter Seven

1. Tyndall, *Forces in Modern British Literature,* 47.

2. *Letters to Christopher* (Santa Barbara, Calif.: Black Sparrow Press, 1980), 131; hereafter cited in the text as *LC*.

3. *European Witness* (New York: Reynal and Hitchcock, 1946), introduction; hereafter cited in the text as *EW*.

4. *Learning Laughter* (London: Weidenfeld and Nicolson, 1952), 1; hereafter cited in the text as *LL*.

Chapter Eight

1. MacNeice, *The Strings Are False,* 112.

2. Samuel Hynes, "An Ambassador of Letters," *New York Times Book Review,* 26 November 1978, 9.

3. Bruce K. Martin, *British Poetry since 1939* (Boston: Twayne, 1985), 173.

Selected Bibliography

PRIMARY WORKS

Poetry

Nine Experiments. Hampstead: privately published by author, 1928. Facsimile edition; Cincinnati: Elliston Poetry Foundation, University of Cincinnati, 1964.
Twenty Poems. Oxford: Basil Blackwell, 1930.
Poems. London: Faber and Faber, 1933, 2nd rev., London: Faber and Faber, 1934. Definitive American ed. New York: Random House, 1934.
Vienna. London: Faber and Faber, 1934; New York: Random House, 1935.
The Still Centre. London: Faber and Faber, 1939.
Selected Poems. London: Faber and Faber, 1940; New York: Random House, 1964 (considerably different selection).
Ruins and Visions. London: Faber and Faber, 1942; New York: Random House, 1942 (also contains *The Still Centre*).
Poems of Dedication. London: Faber and Faber, 1947; New York: Random House, 1947.
The Edge of Being. London: Faber and Faber, 1949; New York: Random House, 1949.
Collected Poems, 1928–1953. London: Faber and Faber, 1955; New York: Random House, 1955.
The Generous Days. London: Faber and Faber, 1971; New York: Random House, 1971.
Collected Poems, 1928–1985. London: Faber and Faber, 1986; New York: Random House, 1986.
Recent Poems. London: Anvil Press, 1978.

Fiction and Drama

The Burning Cactus. London: Faber and Faber, 1936; New York: Random House, 1936.
Trial of a Judge. London: Faber and Faber, 1938; New York: Random House, 1938.
The Backward Son. London: Hogarth, 1940.
Engaged in Writing, and The Fool and the Princess. London: Hamish Hamilton, 1958; New York: Farrar, Straus and Cudhay, 1958.
The Temple. New York: Grove, 1988.

Other Books

The Destructive Element. London: Jonathan Cape, 1935; Boston: Houghton Mifflin, 1936.

Forward from Liberalism. London: Victor Gollancz, 1937; New York: Random House, 1937.

The New Realism. London: Hogarth, 1939.

Life and the Poet. London: Secker and Warburg, 1942. Reprint; New York: Haskell House, 1974.

Citizens in War—and After. London: George G. Harrap, 1945.

European Witness. London: Hamish Hamilton, 1946; New York: Reynal and Hitchcock, 1946.

Poetry since 1939. London: Longmans, Green, 1946.

World within World. London: Hamish Hamilton, 1951; New York: Harcourt, Brace, 1951.

Shelley. London: Longmans, Green, 1952.

Learning Laughter. London: Weidenfeld and Nicolson, 1952; New York: Harcourt, Brace, 1953.

The Creative Element. London: Hamish Hamilton, 1953.

The Making of a Poem. London: Hamish Hamilton, 1955.

The Struggle of the Modern. London: Hamish Hamilton, 1963; Berkeley and Los Angeles: University of California, 1963.

The Year of the Young Rebels. London: Weidenfeld and Nicolson, 1969; New York: Vintage, 1969.

Love-Hate Relations. London: Hamish Hamilton, 1974; New York: Random House, 1974.

T. S. Eliot. New York: Viking, 1975.

The Thirties and After. New York: Random House, 1978.

Henry Moore: Sculptures in Landscape. New York: Clarkson N. Potter, 1979.

Letters to Christopher. Santa Barbara, Calif.: Black Sparrow, 1980.

China Diary. London: Thames and Hudson, 1982.

Oedipus Trilogy. London: Faber and Faber, 1985; New York: Random House, 1985.

Journals, 1939–1983. London: Faber and Faber, 1986; New York: Random House, 1986.

SECONDARY WORKS

Bibliography

Kulkarni, H. B. *Stephen Spender Works and Criticism: An Annotated Bibliography.* New York: Garland, 1976. Useful tool. Omits some American editions. Needs updating.

Tolley, A. T. *The Early Published Poems of Stephen Spender: A Chronology.* Ottawa: Carlton University Press, 1967. Lists poems up to 1934 with initial and subsequent publication, also variations.

Books

Cunningham, Valentine. *British Writers of the Thirties.* Oxford and New York: Oxford University Press, 1988. Poststructuralist analysis of the thirties writers, emphasizing their political naïveté and the destructive element in their work.

Hoskins, Katherine. *Today the Struggle: Literature and Politics in England during the Spanish Civil War.* Austin: University of Texas Press, 1969. Depicts the changing attitudes of major British writers on the right as well as on the left during the 1936–39 period. Like Cunningham, a key study.

Hynes, Samuel. *The Auden Generation: Literature and Politics in England in the 1930s.* New York: Viking, 1972; London: Bodley Head, 1976. Essential anatomy of the between-the-wars British writers, exploring individual consciences and collective reactions.

Kulkarni, H. B. *Stephen Spender: Poet in Crisis.* Bombay: Blackie, 1970. Noncritical overview of Spender's poetry.

MacNeice, Louis. *Modern Poetry: A Personal Essay.* Oxford: Clarendon Press, [1938] 1968. Outstanding account of British poetic practices and practitioners in the 1930s. And insider's view that argues for socially committed poetry and promotes Spender and Auden.

Maxwell, D. E. S. *Poets of the Thirties.* London: Routledge and Kegan Paul, 1969. Survey of British poets of the 1930s emphasizing ideology and groupings. This excellent overview concentrates on Spender's social concerns.

Pandey, Surya Nath. *Stephen Spender: A Study in Poetic Growth.* New Delhi: Arnold Heinemann, 1982. Chronicles Spender's search for social and personal values through poetry, introspection, and redemptive action.

Stanford, Derek. *Stephen Spender, Louis MacNeice, Cecil Day Lewis: A Critical Study.* Grand Rapids, Mich.: Eerdmans, 1969. Factually unreliable chapbook with a Christian viewpoint of the Pylon Poets.

Tolley, A. T. *The Poetry of the Thirties.* London: Victor Gollancz, 1975. Emphasizes political and historical background of the period as manifested in the first group of British poets to develop under influence of Freud, Marx, Proust, Eliot, Joyce, and Lawrence.

Weatherhead, A. K. *Stephen Spender and the Thirties.* Lewisburg, Pa.: Bucknell University Press, 1975. Most important study of Spender's earlier poetry. It tries to compensate for critical neglect.

Articles

Fraser, G. S. "A Poetry of Search (Stephen Spender)." In *Vision and Rhetoric: Studies in Modern Poetry.* London: Faber and Faber, 1959, 202–210.

Commends Spender's flexibility, fluidity, and "peculiar, uncomfortable honesty," which links him with "the great romantic poets."

Jacobs, Willis D. "The Moderate Political Success of Stephen Spender." *College English,* April 1956, 374–78. Highly critical of Spender's poetic ability and political tendentiousness, but admiring of his sensitivity and humanity.

Replogue, Justin. "The Auden Group." *Wisconsin Studies in Contemporary Literature* 5 (1964), 133–50. History of the Auden–Spender–Day Lewis relationship from early school days through the 1930s.

Scarfe, Francis. "Stephen Spender: A Sensitive." In *Auden and After: The Liberation of Poetry, 1930–1941.* London: Routledge, 1942. Early, perspicacious, and laudatory. Spender is "the Wifred Owen of Peace."

Seif, Morton. "The Impact of T. S. Eliot on Auden and Spender." *South Atlantic Quarterly* 53 (1954), 61–69. Outdated hagiography of Eliot, but useful for understanding Eliot's great influence on younger poets.

Smith, Elton Edward. "Stephen Spender: The Proletarian Poet." In *The Angry Young Men of the Thirties.* Carbondale, Ill.: Southern Illinois University Press, 1975, 35–68. Accessible study of Spender and others as revolutionaries and romantics.

Thurley, Geoffrey. "A Kind of Scapegoat: A Retrospective on Stephen Spender." In *The Ironic Harvest: English Poetry in the Twentieth Century.* London: Edward Arnold, 1974, 79–87. Outstanding existentialist perspective in Spender. It rates Spender over Auden.

Weatherhead, A. K. "Stephen Spender: Lyric Impulse and Will." *Contemporary Literature* 12 (1971), 451–65. Discusses conflict in Spender's poetry between his desire "to work in the outside world" and his inherent need to spell out a personal lyric. Spender is "one of the purest lyrical talents of the century in English."

Index

The Author

Sanford Sternlicht is professor emeritus of theater and English at the State University of New York at Oswego and adjunct professor of English at Syracuse University. He is the author of the following books: *Gull's Way* (1961), poetry; *Love in Pompeii* (1967), poetry; *The Black Devil of the Bayous* (1970), history, with E. M. Jameson; *John Webster's Imagery and the Webster Canon* (1972); *McKinley's Bulldog: The Battleship Oregon* (1977), history; *John Masefield* (1977); *C. S. Forester* (1981); *USF Constellation: Yankee Racehorse* (1981), history, with E. M. Jameson; *Padraic Colum* (1985); *John Galsworthy* (1987); *R. F. Delderfield* (1988); and *Stevie Smith* (1990). He has edited *Selected Short Stories of Padraic Colum* (1985), *Selected Plays of Padraic Colum* (1986); *Selected Poems of Padraic Colum* (1989), and *In Search of Stevie Smith* (1991).